CU00939504

*sending you
light & joy)
Sun ♡*

HAPPINESS
IS HERE

A 30-Day Guide to Joy and Fulfilment

SUSANNA HALONEN

Copyright © 2018 Susanna Halonen

All rights reserved.

No part of this publication may be reproduced, distributed, or transmitted in any form or by any means, including photocopying, recording or other electronic or mechanical methods, without the prior written permission of the author, except in the case of brief quotations embodied in critical reviews and certain other non-commercial uses permitted by copyright law. For permission requests, write to info@happyologist.co.uk

ISBN: 1977807739
ISBN-13: 978-1977807731

DEDICATION

I dedicate this book to you.
By picking this book up, you're helping me on my
mission to make the world a happier place because
you're making happiness happen for you.
I express my full gratitude to you.

CONTENTS

HAPPINESS IS HERE

Introduction

As the Happyologist®, the most common question I get asked is, "*Are you always happy?*" To this, I confidently respond, "*No, I'm human.*" It took me years to fully understand this question and to respond to it confidently. Why? Because I, just like the rest of society, had totally misunderstood what happiness is.

I thought that being happy is all about smiling and experiencing bliss. I believed being happy meant never experiencing negative emotions. I thought I was supposed to be in a happy state of mind 24 hours a day seven days a week, and express it in an extroverted manner wherever I went. To experience this happy state of mind, I was supposed to be constantly succeeding at what I was doing and reach every single one of my goals in record time. This formula for having a never-ending happy state of mind is supposedly what we are all meant to follow.

In truth, none of these statements are true, but somehow they have become some of the most popularised happiness myths out there. Yet, they do you a big disservice: they hold your happiness back. And that's exactly what they did for me too.

When I believed in these myths, I thought there was something wrong with me whenever I felt low in my mood. I would try to fight it or hide it, which made me feel even worse. I thought being happy was the ultimate purpose in life, and I thought I was at fault when I was unhappy. That is why I have spent so much of my life chasing happiness.

As a child, I chased it through all kinds of different hobbies and sports. As a teenager, I chased it by following one passion obsessively. As a young professional, I chased it by running after silly definitions of success. Yet, none of these approaches worked. They would give me momentary happiness boosts before I came crashing down to my confused, melancholic mood again. It was only when I discovered positive psychology - the science of happiness and human performance - that I started to understand what happiness actually is.

My first interaction with positive psychology was Shawn Achor's highly recommended book, *The Happiness Advantage*. As I read it, my understanding of happiness grew, as did my curiosity to dive deeper. I immersed myself in blogs, articles, and books on the subject, and everything I read further whet my appetite. After doing a face-to-face two-day introductory training in positive psychology, I knew it was to be my next career step.

Whilst building up the courage to take that step, I started to blog about the happiness insights I was learning on the way. I got serious with a career coach who helped me with my confidence and gave me the positive encouragement I needed to hear in order to start making my own path. It is the clarity and confidence I received from that coach that inspired me to become one as well. Within a year of my first coaching session, I had completed a life coaching accreditation myself. After that, I felt ready and I knew it was time to take the leap.

I left my corporate career in marketing, and within a month, was sitting in a classroom starting my Master of Science in Applied Positive Psychology. I was ready to discover all the secrets of happiness. I wanted to use them on myself so I could become happier, and eventually start helping others to feel better too. Early on in the journey, I coined and trademarked the term Happyologist® as I began building my personal brand as a happiness coach. Embarking on my intense year of happiness studies and business building was exciting.

I studied hard, aced my coursework, built my Happyologist® business and transformed from a natural pessimist into a trained optimist. I lost myself, found myself, then lost myself all over again. That's when I started to realise the master's degree would not give me all the answers. It was simply the first step in my lifelong happiness journey. I would continue to learn many more lessons along the way, sometimes from situations I would least expect. Like from Mickey, the new horse I had acquired the same year I started my master's degree. This young, spirited, sensitive soul quickly became a mirror of my soul. He started giving me just as many answers to my happiness questions as the studying did, but only when I learned to listen.

Often, we are so busy looking for answers and wanting them as quickly as possible that we actually forget to listen: to ourselves, to our intuition, and to the world around us. Instead, we demand answers that are clear, concise, and easy to act on. Answers that are definite, with little margin for error or doubt. Answers that are prescriptive and tell us exactly what we should do. Answers that promise some kind of outcome and result. Unfortunately, happiness, like most things, is not that simple. This is also what makes it so special.

Every single human being is a dynamic soul. You are forever evolving and growing, and so too are your preferences, behaviours, thoughts, and emotions. That is why it is so difficult to chase happiness or give a clear-cut answer on how to reach it. We can chase it in a particular way for so long that when we actually get somewhere, we don't want to do it that way anymore. Other times, we chase it so aggressively that we chase it out of our lives. The key to welcoming happiness into your life is letting it be a byproduct of your actions. That is how you bring it into your life in a holistic and meaningful way. That is when you stop feeling the pressure of having to be happy, of having to smile all the time, and of having to always be upbeat and out there. That's how I stopped feeling the pressure of having to be happy all the time as the Happyologist®.

It took me a long time to realise this, and it was not an easy journey, but I feel like I have arrived somewhere good. Somewhere I feel I have self-belief. Somewhere I feel connected to my intuitive side. Somewhere I feel I can find a better balance. This book is the story of my journey there and of the transformative lessons I learned on the way. I have tested, tried, and researched these approaches, and I have simply stopped to listen to welcome others in. I have discovered what works and when.

The thirty lessons I share here are the ones that have been the most impactful for me. These are the lessons I have fallen in love with, and these are the lessons I practice to this day. They organically welcome happiness into my life without a sense of pressure, obligation, or being enclosed. They are the lessons that make me feel free to live my life exactly as who I am. I hope they will inspire you to do the same.

PART I:

HAPPINESS 101

In this first part of the book, I want to give you some Happiness 101. In other words, I want to give you the basics of happiness. I will teach you what exactly happiness is, what it is not, and why it is so important. This is a key foundation for your happiness because understanding the real science behind it is what makes it more achievable. There are too many happiness myths around, and if you let them lead you astray, they will hold your happiness back. That's exactly what they did to me! It wasn't until I did my Master of Science in Applied Positive Psychology, and became the Happyologist, that I truly learned what happiness is and how to achieve it.

Hence, now I want to teach you exactly what I learned. Dive into Day One to get started!

Day 01:

Why is Happiness Important?

*"Success does not create happiness.
Happiness creates success."*

~ Shawn Achor ~

This quote, by Harvard-educated happiness researcher, Shawn Achor, debunks one of the biggest myths around happiness – that success leads to happiness. This is rarely the case whereas happiness always does drive your success. In fact, happiness drives your success in every area of your life.

But, before we dive into the details of that, I want to ask you a question:

How much of your success at work do you think is predicted by your intelligence and technical skills?

A. 25%

B. 50%

C. 75%

How much, do you think, your intelligence, or in other words your IQ, and your technical skills, which are basically the skills you need to be able to do your job, predict your success at work? When I talk about success at work, I'm talking about things like your overall performance, productivity, and career progression. So, going back to the question, which of the multiple choice options would you choose?

Try not to read ahead and see what the answer is. Have a think about it and try and pick the percentage you believe is the most accurate as the answer. I can tell you it's not the last option. Or the second one. In fact, it's the first one, A, at twenty-five percent! What do you think of that?

I admit I was absolutely shocked when I saw this percentage for the first time. I was so surprised I questioned it and had to re-read it, again and again, to confirm I wasn't imagining things. I had no idea that your intelligence and technical skills have such a small role to play, at 25%, when it comes to predicting your success at work.

Equally, I was very curious, probably just like you are, on what is in the remaining 75% that is more powerful in predicting your success at work. According to Shawn Achor's research, the remaining 75% is made up of three things.[1] First, it's about your optimism and the belief that your behaviour matters in the midst of a challenge. Second, it is about your social connections and the depth and breadth of them. And, finally, the third element, is the way you perceive stress. Ironically, these three things not only heavily influence your happiness, but are also heavily influenced by it. When you are happy, you are more optimistic and resilient when faced with challenges.[2] The happier you are, the more likely you are to build deeper, more meaningful connections.[3] Last but not least, the happier you are, the more stress you are able to handle and use as a positive performance enhancer.[4]

Already there you can see how happiness fuels your success at work. In addition, happier people are also reported to be healthier as they are much more likely to engage in health-promoting behaviours and treat their bodies as the sacred temples they are.[5] Happier people are also 31% more productive and three times more creative than unhappy ones.[6] And, going back to the earlier points, happier people are also less stressed and more socially interactive. Overall, you can see how happiness fuels your success in every area of your life – from your career to your creativity and from your health to your relationships. In short, this first lesson is about realising that it's not success that fuels happiness - but happiness that fuels success. Because when you work on your happiness, you are indirectly working on evolving every part of your life.

To put it in simple terms, this is your first lesson on happiness:

Success ≠ Happiness
Happiness = Success

Homework:

This brings me to the first homework I have for you. Every day, you will receive one happiness tip that I want you to practice in your day or a reflective happiness exercise I want you to do after reading this chapter. This so-called "homework" is critical in your happiness journey because it is an action that will welcome happiness into your life. Hence, try your best to do the homework given every day because happiness won't come simply by thinking about it. It will come through the actions you take.

Today, I have a specific reflection exercise for you to do to better connect with your existing happiness:

1. Think of a time when you felt really, really happy. What were you doing?

What were you seeing? Hearing? Feeling? Close your eyes and imagine yourself being back there. Experience that moment again with all your five senses and stay in it for a minute or two.

2. Now imagine what happened next.
How did you perform when you were feeling happy?
How did you perform after you felt this happiness?

The idea here is to be able to identify a time in your life when you discovered that you performed better when you were feeling good. Reflect on that, brainstorm a few situations like it, and really explore how your happiness fuelled your success in those situations.

Day 02:

What is Happiness?

"Happiness is when what you think, what you say, and what you do are in harmony."

~ Mahatma Gandhi ~

These wise words from Mahatma Gandhi lead me to the second happiness lesson I want to teach you. As Gandhi wisely points out, happiness isn't about following a specific formula that's guaranteed to get you to fulfilment. Instead, it's about creating your own formula for happiness by living a life true to you.

It's important to acknowledge that something that makes someone else happy might not make you happy. Sure, there are certain behaviours and certain mindsets that help to fuel your fulfilment – and we are going to dive deeper into these later in the book. But, how you decide to practice and use these behaviours and mindsets in your own life is entirely up to you.

This brings me to another question I want to ask you:

Which of the below items make you happy?

A. *Eating cake*
B. *Doing something challenging*
C. *Wearing a new outfit*
D. *Helping someone else*

Have a think and take your pick. There is no right or wrong answer here. This is simply for you to better connect with what actually makes you happy. Hence, answer this completely truthfully. You can pick any one or more of the options, or even all of them if you believe each one of them genuinely makes you happy. It's entirely up to you.

According to the science of positive psychology, each one of these options has the power to make you happy. They all tap into the types of happiness that you can experience. When broken down into positive psychology terms, there are two distinct types of happiness: hedonic happiness and eudaimonic happiness.[7]

Hedonic happiness is the short term, momentary bursts of positive emotions – ranging from joy to laughter and from delight to contentment, just to name a few. Basically, anything that gives you a short-term positivity boost, gives you hedonic happiness. For me, wearing a new outfit or eating a piece of cake definitely fits into this category.

On the other side, we've got eudaimonic happiness. This is about feeling a sense of meaning and purpose in the long-term. It gives you a deeper, more sustainable, and more fulfilling type of happiness. Doing something challenging and helping someone else boosts this side of the happiness equilibrium because they help you to connect to life in a more meaningful way.

It's important to note that sometimes, the things that give you eudaimonic happiness, can feel bad or difficult in the moment. For example, when you are doing something challenging, it might be frustrating and stressful in the moment. However, after the experience, you realise how it's helped you to grow and develop. This realisation is what makes eudaimonic happiness happen.

Another example of this is parents of newborns. Research has shown that these parents experience a big dip in their hedonic happiness because they are sleep deprived and overwhelmed with the new change in their life. However, they also experience a huge spike in their eudaimonic happiness because they are getting a whole new sense of purpose in their life as they are responsible for this new being.[8]

Hence, if we were to simplify this happiness lesson, it's this:

Happiness = Pleasure + Purpose

Homework:

Today's homework is for you to look at your own life and your own sense of happiness. Ask yourself, what is it that gives you hedonic happiness? Focus solely on this side of the happiness equation as you will dive deeper into your sense of meaning in a later chapter.

So, today, ask yourself this:

1. What are three things that give you any type of positive emotion?

It could be joy, love, contentment or pleasure. It could even be hope, gratitude or kindness. Basically, a positive emotion is any type of emotion that makes you feel good. What are three things that make you feel good?

2. Do one of the positive emotion boosting activities today. If you can't do exactly that, do the next best closest possible thing.

3. How can you incorporate more of these positive emotion boosting activities into your daily life?

Step one of this homework is critical in helping you to connect with your existing hedonic happiness. Step two is essential for you to realise that happiness is in your own hands. Finally, step three is to help you to bring more hedonic happiness into your life.

Simply put, do more of the things that make you feel good.

Day 03:

What is Not Happiness? – Part I

"Happiness isn't the absence of negative emotions,
it's your ability to deal with them."

~ Susanna Halonen ~

This is a quote from me to you that I've become very passionate to share. Why? Because it debunks a huge happiness myth out there. Somehow, somewhere, someone started saying that you shouldn't feel any negative emotions in your life. Apparently, if you want to be happy, there is no space for negativity. Zero, nada, none.

Instead, you're supposed to put a permanent smile on your face. You're supposed to pretend everything is always fabulous. You're supposed to ignore what is going on inside you for real. Really? Hell no! This is so unbelievably wrong, on so many levels, that I don't even know where to start.

Look – you are human. You are meant to feel both the good and the bad. In order to live a full human life, you need the full experience of human emotions. You need both the positive and the negative. Most importantly, you need to allow yourself to feel these without judgement or frustration.

The more you try to suppress or deny the negative emotions you feel, the more toxic they become.[9] The more you try to change your negative emotions, the more power you give over to them. That's when they start to boil up inside you and create havoc, both in your body and mind. So, what is it exactly that you ought to do with them instead?

Simply acknowledge them. Accept that they are there. Look at them rationally, without blowing them out of proportion. When you're ready, and you've made peace with them, you can dive deeper into them.

Ask yourself why you are feeling them. When did they start? What happened when they started? Why do you think you're feeling them? Often, your negative emotions come to the surface when they want to alert you of something important. Perhaps they're telling you that you're on the wrong path and that you need to adjust your sails. Maybe they're coming out to remind you that you have been mistreated and that you need to fight harder for your rights. They will also come out to tell you when you're in danger, when you're stressed, or when something doesn't feel right.

Allow yourself to feel them and ask yourself why you are feeling them. It's this acknowledgement of them that helps you to make peace with them. Then, once you're ready, you can start to explore why you are feeling them and what - if anything - you can do differently in your day or in your life to feel less of them tomorrow.

But, even here, it's important to note that you are not supposed to completely eliminate negative emotions from your life. You are simply meant to feel confident in handling them. Then, when you can do that, you can also enjoy more of the positive emotions when they come your way. To recap, the lesson here is:

Happiness isn't the absence of negative emotions, but your ability to deal with them.

Homework:

Naturally, today I want you to focus on making peace with your negative emotions. And, rather than asking you to do it right here right now, I want you to take this with you into your daily life.

Jot down the questions underneath, or mark this page with the questions and keep it easily accessible today.

1. Whenever you notice a negative emotion today, simply become aware of it.
Don't try to fight it, resist it, deny it or change it. Simply notice it.

2. Give a label to the negative emotion you feel.
Call it stress, or fear, or anxiety, or whatever it is that you are feeling.

3. Say, "I feel stressed", or "I feel anxious". Basically, say, "I feel X", and fill X with the specific negative emotion that you are experiencing in that moment.

Be very specific with step three here. Make sure to say, "*I FEEL stressed*", rather than, "*I AM stressed.*" By saying feel, rather than am, you are creating a separation between yourself and the negative emotion. You are reinforcing the fact that the emotion you are feeling is nonpermanent and that it is not a permanent part of who you are.

This way of processing negative emotions reminds you that you are not it – as in, you are not the negative emotion. Instead, you are simply feeling it. This way of talking about your negative emotions helps you to acknowledge them whilst also giving less power to them.[10] That means they will be easier to manage and quicker to overcome.

Day 04:

What is Not Happiness? – Part II

*"Being happy doesn't mean everything is perfect.
It means you've decided to look beyond the
imperfections."*

~ Unknown ~

I've seen this quote circled in many different spheres, but unfortunately, I cannot find who said it. I'm sorry I can't accredit it to anyone, especially because it's a brilliant one. It taps into another common happiness myth: in order to be happy, your life has to be in perfect order.

This, in essence, is a pretty rare feat in life. Especially, because life is naturally so dynamic and forever evolving and changing. It's almost impossible to keep things in the same state for long, and, hence, perfection isn't exactly natural in life. Personally, I think that is great.

Can you imagine what life would be like if everything would be permanently perfect? You'd have zero challenges on your plate. You'd have nothing to grow and evolve in. You'd have no adventures to take. That, to me, sounds pretty darn boring. Especially because you, as a human being, naturally love to grow and to evolve.[11] You are doing it every day without thinking, and even more so when you are faced with a challenge or any kind of learning experience.

That's why you need to remind yourself that setbacks, problems, and failures don't hold your happiness back. Things not going to plan don't have to make you miserable. Imperfections in your life don't have to stop you from being happy. In the end, it's not the problems in your life that decide whether you are happy or not. It's how you choose to handle them that does.

It's how you choose to react to them, and the mindset you choose to approach them with. Your mindset truly dictates your ability to deal with any problem, and your self-belief influences whether you're prepared to work hard at overcoming them. Even then, it's not about solving every problem or having an answer to every question.

It's about you trying your best. It's about you realising that you cannot tie your happiness to certain outcomes. It's about you accepting that you can be happy regardless of the problems you are faced with. It's about you believing that you can be happy regardless of the outcomes these challenges lead to.[12]

In short, this is the happiness lesson here:

Happiness is not the absence of problems,
but your ability to deal with them.

Homework:

Today, I have another exercise I want you to take into your day-to-day. This is the best way for you to start seeing your problems in a different light. It is also the most effective way for you to start experiencing the sense of empowerment that comes from seeing problems this way.

1. When you come across a problem today, talk to it.
Say to it: "Everything is fleeting, including you."
That's it. Simply notice the problem and accept its impermanence.

2. Notice how you feel when you are doing this.
The most common reaction is to experience more of a sense of calm and confidence when you voice out loud that the problem is fleeting.

3. Ask yourself: What can I do to diminish this problem – OR - turn my attitude into a more positive one when it comes to dealing with it?

If you can't affect the problem, there is no point wasting your energy whining about it. Instead, try and find a more positive perspective to approach it with. This will help you to feel more empowered and to make peace with the problem you are faced with.

Now go - and have a play with your problems. And, try to have fun with them!

Day 05:

How Do You Reach Happiness?

"Happiness is not something ready-made.
It comes from your own actions."

~ Dalai Lama ~

These words, from Dalai Lama, introduce today's teaching beautifully. But, before I say any more, I want to give you another question to ponder. As before, it's multiple choice:

How much of your happiness
is predicted by your circumstances?

A. 10%
B. 35%
C. 75%

This question is to help you to address how much you think your external circumstances influence your happiness. When I'm talking about external circumstances, I mean anything outside your being. For example, this includes your salary, where you live, your

27

relationships, and what job you have. It even includes who your manager is, what fitness class you go to, and where you shop.

With all that said, how much do you think those external circumstances predict your happiness? Choose the percentage you think is valid for you. Alternatively, you can choose the percentage you think is the average for a general population.

The correct answer might shock you, just like it shocked me. According to research, it's the first choice on the list: ten percent. Can you believe it? I certainly didn't when I saw this finding for the first time. I think it's truly incredible! Why? Because this means that what is happening around you doesn't have to influence how happy you are. The state of your life doesn't actually give an accurate prediction of your happiness.

This also means that 90% of your happiness is predicted entirely by you. However, before we dive into exploring what's in this 90%, it's important to say these numbers are estimates. This research is based on an average population, not individual people. That means the happiness of an average population is only 10% predicted by their circumstances.[13]

It's also important to note that the percentages simply predict how happy you are rather than giving an accurate reading. This means that the percentage split does vary from individual to individual. But, most importantly, the way it is split, with your circumstances playing the least influential part in your happiness, still stands.

When it comes to splitting the remaining 90% that predicts your happiness, there are two key components. Around 50% of your happiness is predicted by your genetics. That means that your genes and what you've inherited from your parents does influence your happiness set level. But, most importantly, the remaining 40% is based on your actions and thoughts. This 40% is what I want you to focus on. This 40% is what this book is about. It's about getting in control of your actions and your thoughts so that you have the maximum chance for happiness.

I want to reiterate again that only 10% of your happiness is predicted by your circumstances. That means now is the time to stop thinking, *"I'll be happy only when I get that promotion"*, *"I'll be happy only when I get married"*, or *"I'll be happy only when I buy a house"*. Because those statements are all myths. Sure, of course you will feel proud when you get that promotion. I'm confident you'll be full of love and excitement on your wedding day. I don't doubt that buying a house will also make you feel good. But then, quickly after each of those instances, you adapt to your new situation and return to your usual happiness set point.

That's why it's so important for you to learn to manage your thoughts and actions. When you learn to do that, you can be happy regardless of the circumstances you are faced with.

That is the fifth and final lesson that lays the foundation for your happiness: believing you can choose it:

Happiness is a daily choice - not a destination.

Homework:

Naturally, that brings you to today's exercise. It's a series of two questions I want you to reflect on:

1. What is one thing you can do to remind yourself to choose happiness daily?

2. What can you do to remember <u>not</u> to chase happiness in the shape of destinations?

Reflect on this, brainstorm it, journal about it, or even sketch about it. Do whatever you need to do to get the answer out of you.

Personally, I have to check in with these questions almost daily. As an ambitious, goal-driven, go-getter, I can get obsessive about going after my goals. Sometimes so much so that I forget to enjoy the journey. That is why I take the time daily to practice mindfulness. Some days it's in the shape of taking a mindful walk, and other days it's doing a guided meditation. I let my mood dictate what shape of mindfulness I need on that particular day and that is what reminds me to choose happiness. The act of being mindful brings me peace and contentment in an instant.

When it comes to the second question, it's about reminding myself to enjoy every step of the journey. If things don't go as planned or things take longer than expected, I simply remind myself it's all part of the journey I'm meant to take.

Now, it's your turn. Go and reflect on these two questions in whatever way that works for you. Then, action your learning and make that reminder happen, every single day. That is how you choose happiness with confidence.

PART II:

YOUR UNIQUE HAPPINESS

This part is all about making your happiness your own. As you learned in part one, there isn't a one-size-fits-all formula for happiness. That's because you are individually so unique. That's why a big part of happiness is understanding who you are and owning up to it. When you're able to connect to your authentic self and be comfortable and confident in your own skin, you naturally start to live a more fulfilling life. You're clear on what is meaningful to you and, hence, you make choices in your life that are aligned with who you are. This will drive your happiness and sense of fulfilment from all angles. That's why this part is about doing a deep dive into your authentic self. It's time to start celebrating you for who you are.

Day 06:

Connect with Your Authentic Self

"To be yourself in a world that is constantly trying to make you something else is the greatest accomplishment."

~ Ralph Waldo Emerson ~

I couldn't agree with these words of Ralph Waldo Emerson any more than I do. They really hit the nail on the head in one of the biggest challenges in today's world. It feels increasingly difficult to stay true to who you are when there is so much noise all around you.

People, companies, and social media accounts are all shouting at you. They're asking you to be more like this or less like that. Every advert you see, every sponsored post on social media you come across, and every comment someone says is telling you to be a certain way. Every bit of feedback you hear and every opinion that gets shoved your way make being you more challenging than ever. And, with today's obsession on social media, it makes it even harder for you to distinguish who is it that you really are, and what is it that you are saying simply because you think it will get more likes.

It's a tricky world out there, but there is no point

whining about it. You've got to take control back and to learn to reconnect with the true you. The full true you. The good and the bad. The perfect bits and the imperfect bits. All of it. Most importantly, don't be afraid of any of it. I know... Easier said than done, right? I totally agree.

I'm the first to admit that I've struggled a lot with this. And, I'm still not perfect with it. Sometimes, I still have days or time periods when being me feels impossible. But, with practice, it's become much easier than it used to be. Before, I used to have moments when I was embarrassed by who I was. I had situations where I hid parts of myself and my life in order to try to protect them from criticism.

Sometimes, I held my tongue back when I should have spoken up. Other times, I refused to let people in when I should have made them my best friend. Why? Because I was afraid of how people perceived me. I was afraid of being told I'm not good enough. I was afraid of showing up fully and getting hurt. And to this day, I still sometimes am. You might be too. And that's ok. That's a part of human nature. You want to feel loved, accepted, and like you belong. Misleadingly, you think that pretending to be a certain way will help you to do that. Yet, really, it only makes it more difficult.

From today onwards, I want you to stop hiding like I did. I want you to push through your fears and show up fully. Because people will listen to you. People will connect with you. And people will ask you to say even more.

The more real you are, the more love you will feel. The more real you are, the more your life will succeed. The more real you are, the more happiness you'll experience.[14]

Today, practice being real. Because the world deserves and desires to see the real you.

Homework:

To help you to connect to your realness, I'd like you to reflect on two specific questions today:

1. When do you feel most like yourself?
When do you feel really true to who you are? When do you feel like you can really show up fully? What environments encourage you to be real?

2. Why? Why do these situations bring your real self out?
What is it about them that makes it possible? What is it that gives you the courage to be you in these situations?

For example, for me, I feel most like myself when I'm delivering a talk. I love being on stage and sharing my message with the world. I love speaking my truth from the bottom of my heart because I believe it has the power to heal. I feel confident being on stage because I have been asked to be there to share my message, and I feel clear that this is exactly what I'm meant to do.

I also feel most like myself when I'm on my horse. He doesn't judge me and accepts me exactly as I am. He brings me to the present, automatically makes me mindful of the moment I am in, and connects me to my intuition.

Now it's your turn. Reflect on these two questions. Discover when you feel most like yourself and why. Uncovering the answers and understanding them will help you to better reconnect with yourself and rediscover those moments of pure authenticity.

Day 07:

Discover Your Values

*"Values are like fingerprints. Nobody's are the same,
but you leave them all over everything you do."*

~ Elvis Presley ~

I love this quote, from the legendary Elvis Presley, for two reasons. First, he points out how your values are completely unique to you. Second, he also highlights that you leave them all over everything that you do. This is exactly right. If you live your life by your values, you take them everywhere you go. You make it clear, both to yourself and to others, which values matter to you the most.

Your values are one of the things that turn you into your most unique self. They are the principles that you want to live your life by. They are the ideologies and standards of behaviour that you find most important. They are the non-negotiable musts in your life, and they are the drivers of your most important decisions. That's why it's so important to be aware of what they are.

When you are clear about your most important values, you can live your truest life. You make decisions that are aligned with who you are and you prioritise the things that most matter to you. Most importantly, you connect with your full being in a more meaningful way.[15]

Your values often become clear when you are faced with a big decision that affects your lifestyle and your long-term path. This is when you tend to weigh your options against your values. For example, my top values are expertise, passion and gratitude. This means that I'm driven by learning and growth and by becoming the best, most knowledgeable version of myself in the different things I do. I am also very committed to living a life that brings my positive passion energy out and is aligned with who I am and what I enjoy doing. Finally, I relish taking the time to appreciate every little aspect of my life and I love showing my gratitude to others too.

Recognising your values like this helps you to take them with you wherever you go. It also helps you to build a life that's coherent with them. Sometimes, the first step of awareness can already light up your joy as you realise you've subconsciously made decisions based on your values and built a life aligned with your true self. Other times, simply asking yourself how you can take these values with you wherever you go can help you to realise how you can make minuscule changes that lead to big effects. Sometimes, all that's needed is a shift in perception or perspective. With that said, it's time to start exploring your values.

Homework:

Today, you have three questions on values to help you to connect to your real self:

1. What are your top three values?
Think about the principles you want to live your life by. What are the non-negotiable ones for you?

To help you to identify your values, here is a list of some values:

- *Achievement*
- *Adventure*
- *Balance*
- *Boldness*
- *Compassion*
- *Creativity*
- *Fairness*
- *Fun*
- *Gratitude*
- *Growth*
- *Honesty*
- *Humour*
- *Independence*
- *Leadership*
- *Learning*
- *Openness*
- *Passion*
- *Purpose*
- *Recognition*
- *Respect*
- *Service*
- *Wisdom*

Feel free to take all three of your values from this list, one or two, or none. Do not feel obliged to take any if none of these is calling out for you. They are simply there for inspiration and idea generation. Of course, if one, two, or three of them jump out at you, use them! But, most importantly, be clear about what each of those words actually means to you, and how you want them to manifest in your life.

Once you've done this, move on to question two.

2. How are you living life in alignment with them now?

What are you doing in your life already that is aligned with your values?

3. How could you live your life more in alignment with your values?

Brainstorm the answers to these questions in any way you want. They will help you to embark on a clearer, stronger path of authenticity. Good luck - and enjoy!

Day 08:

Realise Your Why

"He who has a why can bear almost any how."

~ Friedrich Nietzsche ~

This quote is from one of my favourite philosophers, Friedrich Nietzsche. It's beautiful, isn't it? It's also very relevant to what I want to talk about next: your why.

Before we dive into your why, let me tell you about mine. I'm naturally a very motivated person. I like to set goals, I like to work hard at them, and I like reaching them as much as I enjoy the journey towards them. But there is one thing that makes me even more motivated and even more driven by the goals I set. That is: knowing my why.

Which is exactly why I urge you to know your why. For yourself, your work, and your life. For every single action that you do. Because if you don't know why you're doing it, you should question why you're wasting any time or energy on it. Everything in your life should have a clear purpose – even if that is pure enjoyment. Knowing that purpose behind every action is what makes it easier to prioritise, plan and make time for fun.

It also gives you direction, determination, and resilience in whatever you do.[16] Because when you know why you do what you do, you're much more likely to fight through challenges and bounce back from setbacks. That's why you should make it a habit to ask yourself this: *Why do you do what you do?*

It's that simple, really. *Why do you do what you do?* Direct this question towards your life, your job, or a specific task that is annoying you. Don't get daunted by the idea that in order to have a why, you need to be curing cancer or abolishing poverty. You don't need to be solving some massive humanitarian issue in order to feel a sense of purpose. If you do work in these areas, great! But do also know that a sense of purpose isn't limited to them.

Having a sense of purpose is you simply knowing your why and what is meaningful to you.[17] What is it that makes your life worthwhile? What is it that makes you jump out of bed in the morning? Knowing this overarching why will help you to feel empowered. Knowing the specific whys behind everything you do will help you to connect with those actions in a more meaningful way. Together, your different set of whys will help you to make stuff happen.

This is especially powerful when it comes to connecting to your work in a more meaningful way. For example, if you think your work is just a way to pay your bills and nothing more, then it's just a job to you. If you connect with your job and understand why you do it, that's when it starts to become a career. Last but not least, if your work is something that gives you your sense of purpose and plays a big part in living a meaningful life, that's when it becomes your true calling. And, funnily enough, the more purpose you feel at work, the more passionate, motivated, and happier you are there too.[18]

For example, when I started my first job as a part of the Sony Europe Graduate Scheme, I was over the moon. I was eager to learn, I was hungry to grow, and I admired the company immensely. This was when my work was definitely a career. I felt connected to it, I loved the challenges, and I felt like I was making a difference by trying to help the company evolve.

However, after a few years, when I had been trying to change the status quo and had become frustrated with the slow pace of the corporate world, I lost my connection to it. I no longer felt like the work I was doing had meaning and, hence, it just became a job that paid the bills. This was the opportune timing for positive psychology to enter my life as it did.

Today, being the full-time Happyologist® is my calling. I'm on a mission to make the world a happier place and it's this sense of purpose that drives me in everything that I do.

It's also possible for your sense of purpose to fluctuate at work – or in life. Some days might feel incredible and others will feel more challenging. That, again, is ok. The key is to remain aware of this and to remind yourself of your why when things are feeling tough. This will already start to ease the pressure and help you to better connect with your fulfilment.

Homework:

Now I want you to have a go at exploring your very own unique why. Again, I have a two-step reflection exercise here:

1. Why do you do what you do?
Think both big and small. Think of your overarching life purpose. Think of all the little things you do daily and what their whys are.

2. Then, challenge yourself by asking:
How can you have even more purpose in your life?
What can you do to connect with your life purpose more powerfully?
What can you do to connect to all the little actions you do daily in a more meaningful way?

Brainstorm the answers to these today and go bring more purpose into your life. Then, simply enjoy the fulfilling sense of fulfilment that follows.

Day 09:

Embrace Your Strengths

"Everybody is a genius.
But if you judge a fish by its ability to climb a tree,
it will live its whole life believing it's stupid."

~ Albert Einstein ~

These wise words of good old Albert Einstein make me laugh. He always knew what to say to hit the nail on the head, didn't he? It's almost as if he was way ahead of our time in the way he thought and the things he said. It's a shame we haven't taken more of his lessons onboard.

If we're being honest here, our society is built in a way that it is hard to be the fish you truly are and swim in the ocean you want. Our society is built in a way that it's hard to focus on what you do naturally well. From a young age, you are encouraged to obsess about what you do badly so that you can learn to do it well. You are forced to look at your weaknesses and work hard on improving every single one of them. In a way, this is what the general education system is all about: making everyone averagely good at everything. In reality, this is bad for your productivity, it's bad for your happiness, and it's bad for business.

What you should focus on are your natural strengths. Because you have them and they are completely, beautifully unique to you. These are the traits and qualities you should be fostering. When you do, you'll start performing at your best and feeling less stressed – and research has shown this time after time.[19] You'll also feel lighter, happier and freer. By bringing out your real self and putting your gifts out in the world, you will start to help the world progress.

The more you do this, the easier it becomes, and the stronger and happier you become. Do what you do naturally well. Embrace the things people often praise you for. Master the things that you excel in. Play with the things that you do well without barely putting any effort in. These are your strengths and they deserve to be in the limelight.

Focus on what you do best – and, whenever possible, delegate or simplify the rest. You are meant to use the unique set of strengths that you have been gifted with. And, as a bonus, using them will not only make you happier but also help you to grow and be more productive.

Homework:

Now it's time to dive deeper into your very own strengths. Here are the questions I'd like you to reflect on today:

1. What are your top three strengths?

Get real here about the actual human strengths you have.

Try to forget the technical skills that you've learned along the way, or try to see how they are tied to your innate strengths. What is it that you do that comes naturally to you? What is it that you've often been praised for – yet you've barely even noticed you've done anything special? What is it that makes you come alive? What qualities do you yearn to use? Your strengths should tick the boxes on all those things.[20]

For example, are you naturally good at building rapport with people and earning people's trust? Or are you excellent at seeing both perspectives in a challenge and proffering an effective solution? Or are you the bubbliest, most positive person in your tribe? Or are you simply a superb communicator that always gets their point across clearly and coherently? Those are just a few ideas to get you brainstorming your own unique strengths.

Then, when you're ready, dive into question two.

2. How could you use your strengths in new, different ways?

Could you use them in a different setting? Or in a different scenario? Or could you use them in a different way altogether? What about teaching someone else something about your strengths? This is important because research has shown that the more creative you get with your strengths, the more fun you have and the more productive you are.[21]

Hence, go play with your strengths - and have fun with them!

Day 10:

Unlock Your Passion

*"Break free from the one-passion myth and
embrace your whole life passionately."*

~ Susanna Halonen ~

These words, ironically, are from my book, *Screw
Finding Your Passion*. As the title suggests, I don't
believe in the myth that you are supposed to 'find your
passion' and 'follow your passion' in order to be happy.
In fact, I tried this, multiple times, and every time I
failed.

Take my teenage years as an example. I've loved
horses since the age of 9, and when I was in high school
trying to decide what career path to take, I thought
anything related to horses was meant for me. I thought
that because I loved horses, they were the one passion
that I had found and the one passion that I was meant to
follow. Hence, I actually went to a horse university to
prepare myself for my path – and yes, I promise,
universities offering horse education do exist!

As I started my degree there, I quickly realised it
wasn't right for me. Within weeks of being there, I felt

unfulfilled, anxious, and lost. Worst of all, being there started to kill my love for horses – the one thing that has always brought me joy. That's when I knew I needed a different approach. I left and went to do a standard business degree whilst keeping my horses on the side as a hobby. That seemed to work. It felt good.

Eventually, I graduated with my business degree and got a job in the corporate world. Following a few years there, I felt I had zero passion. I simply couldn't get my passion formula right! Fortunately, as I got more and more fed up with my corporate role, I got more and more fascinated by positive psychology. It came into my life exactly when I needed it the most. After exploring it for over a year, I took the leap to leave my corporate job and I went to do a Master of Science in Applied Positive Psychology.

In it, I had to do a big research project on a topic of my choice. Initially, with the corporate world still very fresh in my mind, I thought my research should be on that. I presented my idea for my research in the corporate space and my supervisor said, "*You must be really passionate about this.*" That's when I thought to myself, "*Hell no!*" and realised this was the perfect opportunity for me to get clear on passion.

Hence, passion is exactly what I researched - and the findings blew me away. I discovered that you can live a more fulfilling life by living your whole life with passion.[22] I discovered you don't need to limit your passion to one activity or a few things. Instead, you can take your positive passion energy wherever you go.

More specifically, I discovered there are five elements that make this possible. The first is all about being your authentic self. As you know, this is something we already covered earlier in the book. The second is knowing your why – again, something that we've explored. The third is seeing your life as a journey of learning. This, on the other hand, is coming up in the next part.

The fourth is knowing your tribe and connecting to it. We've got a whole part of the book dedicated to relationships so you'll find out all about this then. Finally, the fifth is playing with your unique strengths – again, something we just covered. The magic of these five elements is that whenever you take them with you wherever you go and inject them into whatever you do, you are taking your passion with you too.

Homework:

In today's homework, I want you to start connecting with your positive passion energy better. Start this process by asking yourself:

1. When do you feel you are most passionate and energetic?

Don't limit yourself here. Do a proper brainstorm of the different things that make you feel passionate. Is it doing one of your favourite hobbies? Is it being in flow doing something you're really good at? Or is it simply when you're helping others? The answers are entirely unique to you so get clear on what it is that fuels your positive passion energy.

Then, follow on with this question.

2. How can you bring more of that passion into other areas of your life?

Use the five passion elements - your authenticity, purpose, desire to learn, connectedness, and strengths - to unlock that positive passion energy within you. Let it come out of you in multiple ways in multiple settings. Do it, and enjoy the sense of freedom and positive energy that comes with it.

PART III:

YOUR PERSPECTIVE

In part one, you learned happiness is a daily choice you make, not a destination you reach. But how do you actually make this choice? And how do you make it daily? These are the questions that you will get the answers to next.

You'll be learning how being able to choose happiness is all about choosing your perspective. Your happiness is less about what happens to you and more about how you choose to react to what happens. That's why I'm introducing five different practices that help you to have a positive perspective, regardless of what is going on in your life. These practices will help you to see the world through a whole new lens and find fulfilment in places you never thought was possible.

Day 11:

Be Grateful

"It is wise not to grieve for the things you don't have but to rejoice for the things you do have."

~ Epictetus ~

These wise words from philosopher Epictetus summarise the beauty of gratitude. I have to admit, I have a massive soft spot for gratitude. Why? Because it was one of the practices that saved me.

Believe me when I say that I wasn't always this happy. Before I became the Happyologist, I wasn't the happiest, most positive person to be around. In fact, one of the main reasons that led me to enter the world of positive psychology, was because I was so unhappy.

I've always been a little bit of a natural pessimist and being an obsessive perfectionist didn't help that. I used to see the glass as being half empty rather than half full. I used to feel nothing I ever did was 'perfect' enough. It was really exhausting living life this way.

It wasn't until I entered positive psychology and discovered the gratitude practice that I started to change. It transformed my perspective. I started seeing the world through a whole new lens. I started to appreciate myself on a whole new level, including my talents and even my weaknesses. I started to appreciate my lifestyle, from being surrounded by supportive loved ones to having comfortable housing, hot showers, and nutritious food. I started to even appreciate the challenges that came my way and the lessons that came from my missteps. I saw everything in a new light. In short, appreciation changed my life.

Which is exactly why I'm here telling you about it today. It has the power to do the same for you. If you learn to foster an attitude of gratitude, it can change everything. You'll have a healthier, more positive perspective on everything in your life. You will be more appreciative of yourself and more forgiving towards your mistakes. You will be more confident in the beautiful qualities you possess. You'll feel more upbeat and energised, and you'll even be more likely to make healthier choices for yourself.[23]

Homework:

To take your first step into practising this attitude of gratitude, I have one simple question for you:

*What are three specific things you
are most grateful for in the last 24 hours?*

It really is as simple as that. Just answer this question. Write down the three things that you are most grateful for in the last 24 hours.[24] Make sure each item is specific to something that happened over the last 24 hours, rather than something general.

For example, rather than saying you are grateful for your partner, say that you are grateful for the nice sit-down meal you had with them because you both managed to get home from work on time. Rather than saying you're grateful for your body, say that you are grateful for how you managed to push through the whole yoga class you went to, showing your physical strength and your appreciation for your body. Don't worry if it's hard to come up with these three things to start off with. The more you do it, the easier it becomes. Just stick with it.

If you really want to turn gratitude into a habit – which I highly recommend (as you've probably already gathered) - just repeat this question every evening. Every day, finish the day by writing down the three things you were most grateful for in your day. Do it every evening for at least four weeks to start turning it into a habit. When you start to notice yourself looking for things to be grateful for throughout your day, that's when you know the habit building is starting to happen. Then, just keep at it to really make it stick.

Now go, and enjoy a life of gratitude. It's a practice you won't regret.

Day 12:

Practice Optimism

"I could care less if the glass is half full or half empty as long as I can fill it up."

~ Shawn Achor ~

Shawn Achor, the author of *The Happiness Advantage*, introduced me to positive psychology and opened the door to my happiness. That's why today, as we talk about optimism, one of the other mindset practices that changed my life, it's only fitting we start with his words.

Many people believe that it's important to distinguish whether you see the glass as half empty or as half full. However, it's actually more important to think about whether you believe you can fill it up. That's what optimism is all about. And, like gratitude, it's one of the brilliant habits that can change your life.

Optimism has the power to up your motivation and strengthen your resilience. It makes it easier for you to spot opportunities, come up with new ideas, and keep going despite setbacks.[25] It even fuels your gratitude, and gratitude fuels your optimism right back. Most importantly, it turns you into a rational, proactive, solution-focused human ready to take on the world. And that is one of the key lessons I want to give you about optimism.

Being optimistic isn't about denying facts or becoming blindly positive. Instead, it's about acknowledging every challenge rationally and embracing a solution-focused mindset to overcome it. Dr Martin Seligman, one of the founding fathers of positive psychology, recommends three questions to bring that optimistic perspective in.[26]

Whenever you are faced with a problem or a challenge, ask yourself: "*Is this problem permanent?*" Is it always going to be here? Is it never going to disappear? The answer is always no. Because you know that nothing in life is permanent. Even if the situation seems permanent, like losing your job or breaking up a relationship, how you feel about it is not permanent. With time and healing, you will feel better about it. Hence, it is not a permanent problem.

Second, ask yourself: "*Is this problem that you're faced with all-encompassing?*" Does it mean everything is going wrong? Does it mean you have nothing going right in your life? Now, I know it's easy to blow things out of proportion whenever you are faced with a problem. It's natural for you to start exaggerating when you are faced with a problem that seems to take over your whole life and seems to affect how you see the whole world. This question is especially important in situations like this.

Acknowledge that this problem doesn't mean the

whole world is ending and that everything is going wrong. Separate and compartmentalise it, and realise this problem is limited to this area only. Had a bad day at work? It doesn't mean every day at work is bad. Had an argument with a friend? It doesn't mean all your friendships are going wrong. Take a step back and realise that.

The third and final question for you to reflect on is this: "*Is this problem personal?*" Is it all your fault? Is the whole world against you? Here, again, the answer is no. Even if you made a mistake or suffered a setback, it doesn't mean that there weren't multiple variables at play. You did the best you could with the knowledge you had at the time. Realise that the problem isn't a reflection of you being stupid or incapable of doing things. Instead, it's an opportunity for you to learn and grow.

These three questions devised by Dr Martin Seligman are key in helping you to foster an optimistic mindset. As you can see, it's not about ignoring reality or passing blame to someone else. Instead, it's about taking a positive, proactive mindset towards the situation that's challenging you.

Homework:

Today, I want you to take these three questions into your day-to-day life. Whenever you are faced with a problem or challenge today, or even just a situation that's frustrating you, use these three questions to become aware of your mindset:

1. Is this problem permanent?

2. Is this problem all-encompassing?

3. Is this problem personal?

Use these questions to change your mindset into a more positive one. Then, once your mind is in a better state, you'll be able to think more creatively and get more solutions for it, as well as feel more empowered to get on with it.

If you want to practice having an optimistic mindset right now before going into your day-to-day, try this exercise:

1. Pick a problem or a challenge you have.
(If you can't think of any right now, make one up!)

2. Talk about the problem as if you were a pessimist.
i.e. The problem is permanent, all-encompassing, and all my fault.

3. Switch to the other side and talk about it as if you were an optimist.
i.e. The problem is fleeting, it's only this thing rather than my whole life, and there are multiple variables at play, hence, it's not a reflection of me or my abilities.

4. Reflect on the two states of mind you tested out. Which one of them makes you feel more empowered?

I'm going to take a not-so-wild guess and say the optimistic perspective is the one that brings the empowerment in. And, yes, there is plenty of research that agrees with this. Do, however, remember to be kind to yourself even when you notice your pessimistic side kicking in. It's natural for some things, situations or people to bring the pessimist out of you. Simply become aware of it so that you can start to manage it more effectively, and, when you're ready, start massaging it into the optimistic direction.

As a natural pessimist that transformed into a trained optimist, I can tell you it's totally worth it. Now go and practice this today. Fill up your glass with your very own optimism jug.

Day 13:

Notice the Beauty

"Beauty is in the eye of the beholder."

~ Ancient Proverb ~

This ancient proverb is beautifully simple yet so powerful. And you need to be reminded of it. Too often, especially when you're feeling stressed or doubtful, you only see the ugly things.

You see the things that you think don't look good. You see the things that are going wrong. You see the problems and the challenges, rather than the things that are going right. That's why I believe you need to practice your ability to notice the beauty in order to actually see it.

Just like gratitude and optimism, it has the power to shift your perspective and enable you to enjoy life more. In fact, it's something that research has already shown. When you look at beautiful things, you feel happier and more fulfilled.[27] How's that for a happiness hack? Simply look at things that look good! But in all seriousness, I want you to practice this.

I want you to explore what you think is beautiful, and

when and where you usually see that beauty. For me, there is one particular place I really see the beauty like nowhere else. Luckily, it's somewhere I go quite a bit as I have family there. The air is so fresh, the views are incredible, and the nature is mesmerising. It's like you're seeing, inhaling, and experiencing beauty with your full body and being. This happens to me every time I go to Switzerland.

The alpine views, their frosty trees, and the snow covered ground in winter wonderland really make me melt. It stands out to me because I'm not used to seeing it. This happens often. You are more likely to notice the beauty in environments that you are not used to because of the novelty factor. It's new and, hence, your senses are heightened, and as a result, you simply notice more.

However, just because it's harder for you to notice the beauty in your day-to-day life doesn't mean you shouldn't put any effort into it. In fact, it's quite the opposite - you should put more effort in! For example, for me, I see the beauty in more of the details when I look for it in London, where I live. The old lady giving a treat to her dog. The toddler laughing in the swing. The smile of my partner. The edible flower in my favourite cocktail.

When you seek the beauty, you will find it. It is literally everywhere when you open your eyes to it. It is in you and in your surroundings. It is in your eyes and, hence, anywhere you want to look. Let your heart guide you to the beauty you seek. Let that beauty inspire you in all shapes and forms.

Homework:

Today, I have two different exercises for you. The first one, we will do together right here. The second one, you will take into your day.

Let's start with the first:

1. Look up from this page into your surroundings.

2. What can you see around you that is beautiful (perhaps in its own way)?

For example, I can see the tips of the trees from my nearby park when I look out the window. I love their luscious look and I love the autumnal shade they are currently getting. I can see my newly painted nails on my keyboard which shine with sophistication as I type away. I can see a vase with a flower on my shelves. Its pink hue is a nice contrast to the rest of the neutral Nordic colours in my decor.

Now it's back to you. What can you see? Simply look around and notice the different elements and the beauty they possess.

Once you've done this, it's time for the second exercise:

Today, as you go on with your day,
look for the beauty around you.

Be aware of what you see. Try to look at everything - from what you wear to the people you see to the food on your plate to the surroundings around you - with a new 'beauty lens' in focus. See if having this new lens makes you see things differently today.

If it does, keep using it. Actively look for the beauty that lights your soul up. Put the effort in and you will start seeing it all around you.

Day 14:

Do Something Challenging

"If we only did things that were easy,
we wouldn't learn anything.
We'd just practise things we already knew."

~ *David Dockterman* ~

Honestly, how boring would it be to simply practice things we already knew? Never to learn, never to grow, never to try anything new? Personally, it's definitely not my cup of tea. That's why next I want to talk about how you can foster the right mindset to make learning easier and more fun for you.

This is a lesson that is very dear to me. When I learned this myself, it changed my perspective on a lot of things, especially when it came to facing difficult challenges. I learned it in one of my first lectures when I was studying for my Master of Science in Applied Positive Psychology. It really shook me – in the best possible way. Why? Because it was exactly what I needed to hear. I needed to hear that I needed to believe in growth.

There I was, in one my first positive psychology

lectures, way out of my comfort zone. I was doing my first master's degree and I hadn't been in a classroom for years. I was in the new field of psychology, a field I hadn't been involved in since high school. I needed to hear growth was possible because I desperately needed to grow to survive and to thrive in my master's degree studies. I was so fortunate that one of my professors, Dr Kate Hefferon, did a profound session on Carol Dweck's growth mindset.

Dweck says that when you foster this growth mindset, rather than fostering a fixed mindset, you are much more likely to succeed and be more fulfilled.[28] In short, someone with a growth mindset believes that intelligence isn't fixed and neither are any of your abilities. Someone with a fixed mindset, on the other hand, thinks that your intelligence and your abilities are fixed and that they cannot be developed.

As I was listening to the lecture on this, I realised how some situations brought the growth mindset out of me, whereas other ones brought the fixed mindset out. That's when I realised I had to become better at fostering my growth mindset to up my happiness and my likelihood of success.

Why? Because when you have a growth mindset, you bravely open up to new challenges rather than shy away from them. You push yourself to grow rather than hold yourself back. You see setbacks as great lessons rather than failures. Most importantly, you are more fulfilled knowing that you are developing yourself every single day.

To practice having a growth mindset, believe that you can develop in any ability. Believe that effort is the path to mastery. Believe that you can learn from your failures. Believe that challenges help you to grow the most. In summary, believe in growth – and embrace the challenges that make it possible.

Homework:

Today, I have a question that I want you to reflect on firstly here and then take its answer into your day:

*What is one thing you can do today
that challenges you?*

What is one thing you can do that scares you? That pushes you out of your comfort zone? That makes you grow in more ways than one? It could be trying a new exercise class that you know will challenge you. It could be working on your shyness and having a chat with someone in the coffee shop. It could be approaching new, potential clients at work in a more direct way. It can be in any area of your life that you want. The only rule is that it challenges you, scares you, and makes you grow.

Come up with what it is - and then go and do it. Enjoy the growth that comes with it. Because, as a human being, you are happiest when you are growing.

Day 15:

Choose Resilience

"Mind is everything. Muscle is just pieces of rubber.
All that I am, I am because of my mind."

~ Paavo Nurmi ~

This quote by Finnish Olympian, Paavo Nurmi, takes you back to my Finnish roots. Having spent the majority of my life living abroad, I have to admit my Finnish knowledge is weak. I know we Finns are quiet, and I know we are reserved. I know we love nature and even more so if we can experience it in solitude. Those are the things I know and those are the things I am. And then - there is - *sisu*: the unique Finnish spirit of persistent determination.

When you've hit a wall and all the odds seem against you, *sisu* comes alive. What must be done, will be done, regardless of what it takes. It's a magical-like quality that mixes determination with grit, stamina, perseverance, courage, and resilience. And that's what I want to focus today's lesson on: on having *sisu*. On being resilient. Why? Because you need it if you want to stay strong and be determined on your path.

Earlier in this book, you learned that you can't control what you are faced with. You also learned that you can control how you choose to react to the things that come your way. You learned that happiness isn't about having a perfect life without problems, but about confidently dealing with all the imperfections. If you have resilience, you are stronger in dealing with them.[29]

You don't let setbacks bring you down and you don't let failures stop you from trying. You don't let people's opinions prevent you from going after what you want and you don't let self-doubt hold you back. You know you have everything you need in order to be happy and fulfilled, and you know you will go after anything you want with confidence.

Naturally, you are an incredibly resilient soul. Sometimes, however, it can feel more difficult to tap into it. That's why today I want to remind you that your resilient self exists. It's right there inside of you. Just give it a little nudge and wake it up. It will show up when asked.

Homework:

To reconnect with your resilient self, I have a two-step reflection exercise for you:

1. Think of a time when you were faced with a setback or experienced some sort of failure that felt difficult to overcome.

It doesn't matter if it was small or big, or at work or

in your personal life. Just pick one that was tricky to overcome and that you can remember clearly.

Then, move on to question two:

2. How is your life - or how are you - better because of it? How is your life or how are you better because of this setback?

Let me give you an example. When I was about to leave my corporate career and start my master's degree in positive psychology, I got headhunted by Apple. They wanted to interview me for a potential role with them so I figured I might as well give it a shot. I got blinded by the idea of working for big, shiny, impressive Apple, and I actually started considering postponing my master's degree. Eventually, after rounds and rounds of interviews, they said they loved my profile and my skillset, but they didn't have a fitting role open for me at that point in time. They said they'd keep my CV and get in touch once a relevant role opened up. I was gutted.

I felt like an utter failure and that I wasn't good enough to work for Apple. But, I didn't waste much time. I picked myself up, went to do my master's degree studies as originally planned, and became the full-time Happyologist.

How did my life - or how am I - better because of it? Well, because of their rejection, I got to do the master's degree I wanted to do. I got to enter the field I wanted to enter and I got to set up my own Happyologist business. I got to become the person I am today with a full-time job of helping people to live happier, more fulfilling lives. How's that for a happy twist? Because of that "failure" of not getting the Apple gig, I got my new dream career in being the Happyologist.

Now, it's your turn. What is a setback or failure you experienced? And how is your life - and how are you - better as a result? Go and have fun with this question. It's a great one to go back on, again and again, to remind you of your resilient self. It is there, strong and bold. Sometimes, you just have to remind yourself of it.

PART IV:

YOUR RELATIONSHIPS

As a human being, you are a social creature. That means you need others not only to survive but also to thrive. That's why this next part is all about making the most out of your relationships, both close and far. Since relationships play a big part in your happiness, it's important to know what you can do to ensure they are in their best shape. It's also useful to explore how to deal with relationships that might be holding you or your happiness back, and even learn how to make interactions with strangers more positive. Last, but not least, it's good to be reminded of the most powerful human emotion there is: love. It's my favourite one so I can't wait to share my take on it with you. Now turn the page and start getting the basics of your relationships right.

Day 16:

Connect

"Connection is the energy that exists between people when they feel seen, heard, and valued."

~ Brené Brown ~

These words from Brené Brown highlight the importance of the connections in your life. As a human being, you are a social creature. That means you need the energy and enthusiasm of others in order to fully thrive.[30]

These people might be your family, your closest friends, your partner, or even your colleagues. Maybe they are your dog or your cat or even your horse - like for me it is! It really doesn't matter who they are as long as they are helping you in one way or another.

They might be inspiring you, empowering you, or lifting you up. They might be calming to be around, or their positivity could be beautifully contagious. They might be your biggest cheerleaders and believe in you more than you do so yourself. On a good day, they might be doing all of the above - so let them.

Let them work their magic on you and be aware of

who these individuals are. Invest in these relationships with your whole being. Make enough time to interact and engage with them mindfully. They are all working their magic on you in their own unique way, and, equally, you are doing the same for them.

You give energy back to them as they share their energy with you. You support each other, you encourage each other, and you love each other wholeheartedly. Just as much as you give to them, make sure you let them give to you too. Let them in with your whole heart and connect with them in a fulfilling way. Give them your time, attention, and love.

Leave them better off than when you found them. Let them do the same for you. Let them connect with you and lift you up.

Homework:

Naturally, I want you to think of who these people are. Start this process off by identifying the people who are in your inner tribe:

Who are the people that energise you, encourage you, and believe in you - sometimes more than you believe in yourself?

Who are the people who love you for who you are and encourage you to show up authentically every single day?

Is it your best friend or your partner? Your parent or sibling? Or maybe a colleague who is so much more than simply someone you work with? It could even be your pet! List the people (or animals!) who lift you up and inspire you to connect with your real self, again and again. As you write their names down, give a silent thank you to each and every one of them for being in your life.

Second, connect with one of them today:

Connect with someone in your tribe
in an interactive way.

Make it someone who you haven't connected with for a while, or haven't had an in-depth conversation with for some time. Meet them face-to-face if you can. If this isn't an option, Skype them, FaceTime them, Whatsapp call them, or use an actual telephone. Do something - anything - that makes you have a real conversation with them.

Don't go for the lazy options of texting or emailing them. The energy exchange just isn't the same if you aren't talking to them live and hearing their voice. Better yet, try to see their face, even if it is through a webcam.

To recap, list all the people in your tribe who lift you up first. Second, connect with one of them today face-to-face or through a call. Connect with them and let that magical energy exchange happen.

Day 17:

Be Kind

*"Love and compassion are necessities, not luxuries.
Without them, humanity cannot survive."*

~ Dalai Lama ~

How beautiful are these words from Dalai Lama? Love
and compassion being necessities. Love and compassion
being the keys to your survival. When you think about
it, it's so true.

Not much would work in this world without
compassion, especially your relationships.[31] That's why
it's so important to remind yourself, every now and
again, about the value of compassion - both towards
yourself and towards others.

It's especially critical in today's age. It feels like a
difficult time for humanity, or at least in my eyes and
bones it does. Controversial political results are
happening all around the world, the terrorist attacks just
keep on coming, and the debates and divisions seem to
get bigger and more hostile. It feels like the world has
been going a bit backwards, and you constantly hear
loud, angry messaging that makes my heart ache.

That's why I want to remind you to practice compassion. It's more important than ever because it's more needed than ever. We need to use compassion together to heal ourselves, each other, and the world.

To practice compassion, fill your heart with love and share that love with the world. Show the compassion that you are meant to share. Show compassion not only to your loved ones but also to yourself. Show it not only to strangers but towards all of humanity. Show it to everyone you come across equally - regardless of race, nationality, gender or age.

Show it to those who are feeling lonely, overwhelmed or sad. Show it even to those who are looking joyful, empowered and good. Show it to everyone you meet because they might need it more than you think as you never really know what's truly going on inside someone else.

Treat everyone, regardless of their views or opinions, with equal kindness. Because, in the end, we are all human and we all deserve compassion.

Homework:

Today, I want you to approach your day with the most compassionate heart. To really practice it, I have a little challenge for you:

Do three random acts of kindness today.

That's it. As simple as that. Do three random acts of kindness of your choice. They can be towards people you know, they can be towards complete strangers, or they can be a mix of both.

Try and do something that you don't usually do. For example, buy a coffee for the stranger behind you in the coffee shop queue. Give a homeless person a bag of food and a blanket. Offer to babysit your neighbours' baby so they can go out on a date. Help a colleague with one of their tedious admin tasks. It really doesn't matter what this random act of kindness is as long as it's born from a place of kindness.

Now go and spread that compassion in your world today - and keep it with you for the days to come.

Day 18:

Celebrate

*"The more you praise and celebrate life,
the more there is in life to celebrate."*

~ Oprah Winfrey ~

I'm going to take this quote a step further and evolve it to, *"The more you praise and celebrate the <u>people</u> in your life, the more <u>people</u> there are in your life to celebrate."* This is a strong truth because it's the one thing that helps you to strengthen any bond you have.

When you appreciate the person you have a relationship with and you take the time to celebrate it, you make the bond stronger and more fulfilling.[32] This learning really hit home for me a few years back when I was talking to my beloved Grandma, who was over 90 years old back then. She reminded me how important it is to celebrate people, and life, in general.

I vividly remember the moment I was talking to her on the phone about my approaching birthday. She asked how I was planning to celebrate it and with whom. I said I was going to take it pretty easy and wasn't really planning on celebrating it much. That's when she firmly said, "*There are too many ordinary days in your life. When there is a cause to celebrate, celebrate!*" As usual, she blew me away with her wisdom and this point has stuck with me to this day.

I totally agree with her and think you should make the effort to celebrate more. Not only your birthdays, promotions, or other successes – but actually your loved ones. When was the last time you celebrated a win of theirs? When was the last time you celebrated them simply being in your life? For being there when you needed it the most? For believing in you and for supporting you?

I don't think we do this nearly enough so I urge you to do it today. Because, like my Grandma said, there are too many ordinary days in your life. You can turn today into an extraordinary one by saying a heartfelt thank you to someone you love.

Homework:

This is exactly the homework I want to leave you with today - saying thank you:

1. Pick someone in your life to give thanks to.
Pick anyone you want and get ready to give a heartfelt thank you to them.

2. Tell them what they mean to you. Tell them what you admire and appreciate about them the most. Do this through a face-to-face conversation, a phone call, an email, or even a letter.

Do not just send a text or a Whatsapp message. Don't just post on their Facebook wall or comment on their social media post. Make this private and make this meaningful. Make it so that they feel it in their full being.

If you decide to call them, plan in advance what you want to say. If you write a letter, make it a full page about why you are so grateful to have them in your life.

Be honest. Be appreciative. That's how you make that celebration count.

Day 19:

Declutter

*"Simplicity boils down to two steps:
Identify the essential. Eliminate the rest."*

~ Leo Babauta ~

These clever words on simplifying your life can equally be applied to your relationships. Too often, you try to hold on to relationships that you've outgrown. These might be romantic relationships, friendships, or even relationships with blood relatives. Some of these relationships can be made up of the wrong people.

These are the people who zap your energy and breathe toxicity into your air. They put self-doubt into your head and openly judge the decisions you make in your life. They put a negative spin on everything and say nothing is ever good enough. These are the people you should declutter out of your life.

If you spend a lot of time with them, they will start holding you and your happiness back.[33] Their negative moods will infect you and their judgmental comments will become an echo in your head. You'll start to believe what they have to say and stop living the life you are meant to live.

When it comes to how you declutter them, you have three options. One: you talk to them about how their judgemental comments are bringing you down. You try to work together to come up with a plan on how to make your relationship more positive. If they're worthy of you, they will want to heal the relationship you have. Simply opening up honest communication like this might help them to open up about what they're going through. Perhaps there is an underlying issue that has resulted in them becoming this ball of negativity - and they simply hadn't noticed. That's when you have an opportunity to help them to get to a more positive place and, hence, also help heal your relationship.

The second option is more brutal: you minimise communication with them. You take a breather from meeting them. You stop scrolling their social media feeds. Sometimes, having a break from each other can already calm things down. You can both focus on working on yourselves and regroup when you feel the urge to do so. When you are both up for giving it another go, it might be the mood has already been reset to a more positive one.

The third option is ideal if you have to spend time with them because they are your colleagues or your family or your in-laws. Sometimes you will have to suck it up and deal with the toxic energy they carry. How? By creating a protective bubble around yourself whenever you meet them.

Try to only meet them when you are feeling

energised, positive and strong. Go into the conversations with them with a resilient mindset. Let their comments go in one ear and out the other. Politely decline people's opinions or suggestions if you are not interested in hearing them. Sometimes, the simple act of being open about how you feel, and turning their judgements down, stops them from being toxic. Most importantly, after spending time with them, give yourself some well-earned rest and recharging time.

If none of these options work, it might be time to limit your time with them if you can - or even totally kick them out of your life. Don't give them time and attention if they haven't earned it. Try your best at fixing the relationship and getting them to meet you halfway. But, if you see no signs of improvement or no desire from them to make an effort, let them be. Because in the end, you have to put yourself first and you cannot let other people take your joy away from you.

Homework:

Let's put this into practice. To do that, we are taking decluttering inspiration from Marie Kondo's tidying method.[34] When in doubt about whether to keep someone in your life, use this adapted question to get clear:

Does this person give me joy?

So simple yet so powerful. But how do you navigate the answers?

The easy one is yes, this person does give me joy. Then, definitely keep them, celebrate them, and appreciate them. Make time for them. These are your sources of relationship sunshine.

If the answer is no, and they really don't give you joy, take a breather from them. If deep down you know you have outgrown each other, let them go. You are not meant to be in each other's lives right now. By letting them go, you are also making room for someone else who's waiting around the corner to enter your life. And, who knows, your paths might cross again in the future if the vibe is right.

If the answer is no, they don't give you joy, but yes, you do have to have them in your life because they are family, in-laws, or a colleague, you have to do a bit more work. Ask yourself: how can you make your interactions with them more joyful? What can you do to inject more joy into the relationship? Can you focus on the positives or can you give them more compliments? Can you try to be so positive around them that it starts to rub off on them?

Have a go with a few different strategies and see what happens. If nothing changes or improves after you've tried to inject more joy in, again and again, try to limit your interactions with them. You don't want them to zap all your positivity out of you. If limiting your interactions with them isn't possible, create a strong positivity shield around you and filter the negative comments out. Don't let their bad energy affect you or your heart.

Go and be bold with your cleanse. Declutter or heal the relationships that are holding your happiness back.

Day 20:

Love

*"All, everything that I understand,
I understand only because I love."*

~ Leo Tolstoy ~

These beautiful words from Leo Tolstoy summarise the true source of all your meaningful relationships.[35] Love. L-O-V-E. This incredible four-letter word is one of the most powerful things on our planet. Because, in the end, love is the answer.

Love is always the answer - no matter the question. Love for yourself, love for your loved ones, and love for your community. Love for your successes, love for your lessons, and love for your life. Love not hate, love not anger, love not fear.

When it comes to your relationships – be it romantic ones, friendships, or family ones – love fully and wholeheartedly. Love boldly and unashamedly. Because love has the power to heal anything and to create the strongest, most fulfilling bonds with the people that matter to you the most. Love with confidence and with faith. Give people your loving trust and give them a chance. Let them give the same chance to you. Let them love you back.

Whenever you spend time with someone you truly love and care for, tell them you love them. Show them you love them by being fully present. Do it with meaning and do it with power. Let it warm your soul and the souls of those around you.

Love with your whole heart and being. Open up to it fully. Get ready to feel it – and then feel it. Share it and show it. Embrace it and magnify it. Because, when it comes down to it, life is all about love.

Homework:

I want to give you one simple piece of homework today:

Say this to someone you love: "I love you".

Just look into their eyes and say "*I love you*". Say it to anyone you want to say it to - as long as that love is genuine and true. It could be your partner, your parent, or your sibling. It could be your child, your pet, or your best friend. It doesn't matter who it is as long as you truly love them and you want to tell them so boldly.

So go, and tell someone you love "*I love you*".

PART V:

YOUR BODY

When you're chasing happiness, you can get a little bit lost in your head. From thinking about what you should say to how you should think to what kind of perspective you should practice - I admit it can get a little bit overwhelming. That's why this part is all about getting out of your head and into your body. The next five chapters are about what you can physically do, rather than mentally think about, to become happier. Every chapter is focused on one specific action whilst explaining why that particular action is so powerful and influential in your happiness. I hope you enjoy these bodily tricks, and, most importantly, I hope you test every single one of them in real life!

Day 21:

Breathe

"Breathing in, I calm my body.
Breathing out, I smile."

~ Thich Nhat Hanh ~

I love these words from Thich Nhat Hanh. They beautifully demonstrate the magic of the one thing you do without thinking that keeps you alive: your breath.

Your breath sustains every cell in your body, mind and soul. It makes it possible for you to be here today reading this book. Yet, since you do it without thinking, you forget its power.

If you give it some attention, and really break it down, every inhale and every exhale has a specific purpose. Every time you inhale, you energise your body. Every time you exhale, you relax your body. Every single breath you take taps into your parasympathetic nervous system, affecting how your body and mind feel.[36]

When you take deep, calm breaths, you calm your whole body down. When you take shallow, nervous breaths, you make your body and mind tense up. That's why learning to control your breath will enable you to control your whole body. This, in turn, will even influence your mind.

When you're feeling stressed or anxious, you can change your whole mental state by changing how you breathe. Taking long, calm, deep breaths can lower your heart rate, relax all the muscles in your body, and totally refocus your mind. And, funnily enough, the more relaxed you are, the easier it is to welcome happiness in the natural way.

Homework:

Today, I want you to practice conscious breathing. In order to do that, I'm introducing a specific breathing method by Dr Andrew Weil. He has researched breathing in depth and found a simple 4-7-8 breathing cycle to be incredibly effective when it comes to relaxation.[37]

It goes as follows:

1. Inhale through your nose for 4 counts.
2. Hold your breath for 7 counts.
3. Exhale through relaxed, pressed lips for 8 counts.
4. Repeat again and again until you start to feel the relaxation.

Have a go at it right now. Inhale for one... two... three... four... Hold for one... two... three... four... five... six... seven... And exhale one... two... three... four... five... six... seven... eight...

The more you do it, the easier it becomes. In the beginning, if you want, you can start with shorter periods of holding your breath and exhaling if the full 4-7-8 count makes you tense. However, you should definitely work towards holding your breath for the full seven counts and exhaling for the full eight counts, as these are the two key actions that really help to calm your body down.

Hence, to really nail this practice, your homework is this:

Take three conscious breathing breaks today in which you practice this 4-7-8 method for three breaths each time.

In the future, whenever you are feeling stressed, anxious, or perhaps even nervous before a performance, use this method to calm yourself down. You can even add it to your pre-sleep ritual as it's also effective in treating insomnia and improving the quality of your sleep.

Now go – and just breathe.

Day 22:

Smile

"A smile is the prettiest thing you can wear."

~ Unknown ~

This beauty, by author unknown, is one of my favourite quotes for three reasons. First, it's because I agree with it so strongly. Second, it's because I believe smiling is one of the most powerful, universally understood gestures there is. Third, it's because smiling plays a big part in how you communicate, how you nurture your relationships, and how you feel.

Let's start with the communication bit. According to Dr Albert Mehrabian, only about 7% of your communication is based on words. On the other hand, nonverbal elements, like smiling, take up about 55% of your communication.[38] That means that if you can bring that smile out whenever you are with someone else, you are getting a head start with creating a positive, confident impression of yourself.

This brings me to the second point: smiling and your relationships. When you see someone smile, the mirror neurons in your brain activate automatically.[39] This immediately makes you want to reciprocate the gesture and smile back. That means that whenever you smile, you make it more likely for other people to smile too. You basically have the power to start a positivity spiral around you – as well as connect with people, both close and far, in a positive way.

Which brings me to the third point: how smiling makes you feel. When you smile, you trigger your brain's reward mechanism, making it produce happy hormones.[40] These happy hormones, in turn, make you feel good, which makes you want to smile even more. This results in even more happy hormones in your body. Basically, one smile can totally shift the energy in your body if you let it. And, best of all, even a fake smile can start the happy hormone production. Hence, even if you're feeling frustrated or stressed, forcing yourself to smile can help you to get back into a more positive place.

Homework:

It's probably no surprise to you that today's homework is today's action: smiling! But, before you jump into it, I'm not asking for just any kind of smiling. Specifically, I'm asking you to do this:

Smile at three strangers today.

Yup, that's today's homework: smiling at strangers! Not just smiling randomly to yourself, to your colleagues, or to your family. That would be too easy. Of course, I still encourage you to smile to them anyways.

But, for your homework, I want you to make a real smiling effort.

Why? Because it's useful to practice smiling to new people and doing it also helps to spread positivity around you. The first smile might feel a little bit awkward to offer. The second one will already start to feel easier. By the third, you'll start to enjoy it and want to do it even more.

Don't be put off if someone you smile at forgets to smile back. Even if they didn't show their positive energy shift right then and there, they definitely felt something in their subconscious even if they weren't ready to admit it in front of you.

Now go, and share your beautiful smile with the world. Remember to not let the world change your smile but, instead, let your smile change the world.

Day 23:

Hug

"I have learned that there is more power in a good strong hug than in a thousand meaningful words."

~ Ann Hood ~

This is just it. Who doesn't like a good hug? A cosy cuddle? A loving embrace? I certainly do – with people and animals both! I'm not shy to admit I love cuddling my partner, hugging my horse, and taking dogs on my lap. There's even a scientific reason why I love it so much – and why you probably love it too.

Any type of hug or cuddle gets oxytocin, also known as the "love drug", flowing in your body.[41] This magical oxytocin naturally calms your nervous system down, making you feel less anxious and more relaxed. It also boosts your positive emotions, making you feel more upbeat and empowered. Last but not least, hugging also lowers your blood pressure, putting your body in a happier and healthier state to perform.

All of these benefits spiral into even more goodness by reducing your stress and boosting the quality of your sleep. And those are just the benefits that you feel in your body and being. If you dive deeper, you'll realise that hugging also increases your social connections and gives you a stronger sense of belonging.[42] It can even create stronger bonds with the people you truly care about. Really, it's all good news when it comes to hugs.

If you want to supercharge your hugs, and the benefits that both you and the recipient get, practice giving your best possible hug. First, be present. Don't think about anything else except hugging that person when you hug them. Second, hold them tight. Give them a little squeeze to show that you care and that you mean it. Third, if you're bold enough, hug for at least 20 seconds. Yes, I know that sounds like a long time, but it's well worth it. Research has suggested that 20 seconds is the optimal time to hold a loving hug to get a healthy dose of oxytocin flowing in your body.[43]

Homework:

Today's homework is pretty straightforward:

Give someone a 20-second hug.

It's entirely up to you who that lucky person (or animal!) is. It could be someone you hug a lot or someone you haven't hugged for a while. Whoever it is, they will appreciate it and feel the benefits that follow it.

Go give someone a good, strong hug - and enjoy it yourself too.

Day 24:

Power Pose

"Your body changes your mind, your mind can change your behaviour, and your behaviour can change your outcomes. So – if the goal is confidence – Don't fake it till you make it. Fake it till you become it."

~ Amy Cuddy ~

These words from American social psychologist, Amy Cuddy, sum up the power of your body. Your body uses its body language to communicate externally to others how you feel. However, internally, it also actually influences how you feel.

That's why, with the right bodily tricks, you can actually change how you feel. By changing what you do with your body, you can change your mood. More specifically, there is one thing you can do with your body that can really up your game: the power pose.

I learned the power pose from Amy Cuddy's impressive TED talk.[44] In it, she explains the full story of how she discovered the power pose, the research she's done on it, and how the pose itself has helped her to change her life. It's one of the most viewed TED talks for the right reasons and, hence, I highly recommend you watch it.

For now, I'll give you the quick spiel. Amy did some incredible research which showed that holding the power pose for two minutes before a high-stress situation improves your confidence and boosts your performance.[45] Naturally, when I discovered this, I wanted to test it out myself.

I started to do the power pose before big meetings and before talks in front of thousands of people. I discovered she's totally right. The power pose works. I felt calmer, I felt more focused, and I felt like the stage was mine. I felt invincible.

Now, I do the power pose religiously before every high-stress situation. I'm hooked on it and its positive effects. Sometimes, I even use it in my day-to-day if I'm feeling a bit stressed, anxious or overwhelmed. Even then it succeeds in making me feel better.

Homework:

Naturally, I want you to test out the power pose yourself. First, let me start by explaining how it's done:

1. Stand up.
2. Put your feet firmly on the ground and have them a little bit wider than your hips.
3. Straighten your posture, push your chest out, and lift your chin.
4. Put your hand firmly on your hips - or high above

your head straight towards the sky.
5. Hold the pose for two minutes. Remember to keep on breathing.

Basically, the power pose replicates the Wonder Woman or Superman pose. It might feel a little bit ridiculous and silly at the start, but don't let that stop you. Just keep going and hold the pose.

The key to making this pose as effective as possible is to make yourself feel as big as possible. You want to occupy as much space as you can with your physical body. That's why you're standing tall with your chin up, your feet firmly on the ground, and your hands on your hips. This is what sends the signal of confidence to your brain as your body is saying, "*I'm here, I'm showing up fully, and I mean business*".

When holding the pose for the two minutes, try to stay relaxed. Make sure you don't tense up your body or let your shoulders creep up towards your ears. Instead, take deep breaths to calm your mind and hold everything firmly but softly in place.

Once you've practised doing the power pose, I want you to take it into your day:

Do the power pose for two minutes today.

Do it before an important meeting, when you're feeling stressed, or when you're looking for a confidence boost.

If you feel self-conscious about doing the power pose with people around you, go into a quiet corner or even to the bathroom to do it in your own privacy.

Then, take a deep breath and get into the power pose position. Be focused and fierce, and hold your power pose for two minutes. Hold it, and feel the magic happen.

Day 25:

Move

*"There is no point to samba
if it doesn't make you smile."*

~ Alma Guillermoprieto ~

This quote from Brazilian Alma Guillermoprieto sums up the Brazilian spirit beautifully. Today, I can really see samba for what it is even though initially, I wasn't that keen to understand it.

I moved to Brazil from Finland with my family when I was nine years old. I wasn't exactly thrilled about it at the start. I was a young, insecure girl who didn't speak a word of Portuguese and had no idea where she was going. I was overwhelmed by the megacity of São Paulo, where we moved, and I got a total culture shock with all its noise and chaos. Coming from a tiny little town outside Helsinki, where I lived literally 20 meters from the forest, I was kind of used to peace and quiet.

Luckily, I had my loving parents and three brothers to support me through it. We moved there, we lived there, and... we loved it! It was difficult when the time came to leave it. I had become so immersed in the

Brazilian culture as it wrapped its warm, welcoming spirit around me. I felt like I belonged.

That's why I try to carry the spirit of samba with me wherever I go. Because samba is not just a dance – it is so much more. It's the Brazilian way of having fun, of living in the moment, and of making the most out of every moment. And, I believe, it's also the way you should approach your daily exercise.

The wellbeing industry continues to keep on growing and there are new health, fitness, and yoga coaches popping up left, right and centre. I think this is great… as long as it's all approached with this samba attitude.

When you do your daily exercise, do something that is fun and gives you joy, not something that crushes your soul. Mix it up so you don't get bored of doing the same thing and remember to always samba it up.

It doesn't mean that every bit of exercise is easy and unchallenging. It just means you approach it with an attitude of joy. And, even more importantly, keep moving your body throughout the day.

As a human, you are not designed to sit all day crouching over your desk. Your body is designed to move so keep moving it throughout your day. Stand up regularly, stretch, do plenty of twirls, and share your dance moves with your office. Ideally, according to research, you should move every 20 minutes to keep your circulation going, your mind active, and your energy high.[46] Just do something, anything, to keep moving - and keep that samba spirit alive when you do.

Homework:

Naturally, today's homework is for you to move. More specifically, it's this:

Move at least three times today, and, for 10 minutes each of those times.

Do keep on stretching, twirling, and doing some moves throughout your day. But, also, create these three active sprints of 10-minutes of movement.

For example, your movement could be 10 minutes of yoga in the morning to start your day; dancing to your favourite songs for 10 minutes; going for a short jog; doing some kind of HIIT workout; or, getting it on in the bedroom with your partner - it counts!

It is entirely up to you what those spurts of movement are. The only rule is that you spread them out throughout your day so you move for ten minutes three times.

Have fun with this today and keep on moving!

PART VI:

MAKING YOUR HAPPINESS LAST

As this is the final part of the book, I want to make sure you feel inspired, empowered, and excited to continue your happiness journey. That's why this part is all about how to make happiness stick for good. These are some of my favourite tips and they are the icing on the cake when it comes to making sure that your happiness is meaningful and long-lasting. I hope you enjoy these final tips as much as I enjoyed writing them – they all carry a very special significance to me.

Day 26:

Nurture Yourself

"If you don't take care of yourself,
you can't take care of others."

~ *Susanna Halonen* ~

I repeat these words to myself a lot. When it comes to nurturing myself and taking care of myself, I have had to learn it, and relearn it, and relearn it, time after time. It still isn't easy for me, but it's definitely easier than it used to be.

I'm better at listening to my body, understanding what it wants, and giving it what it needs. And that's just it. You find it so easy to listen to others and give them what they need. You find joy in helping them in any way you can. Yet, when it comes to doing the same for yourself, it can be a real struggle. Especially, if you, like me, like to operate in extremes.

Whatever I do, I do with passion. When I commit, I commit 200%. Whatever I feel, I feel with every cell in my body and being. I fill my calendar with the varied activities I love and I get busy with them. I love living a full and fulfilling life! However, that means that sometimes I struggle to find balance, and end up in burnout.

That's why this is the one tip I need to remind myself of, again and again: to nurture yourself. Because nobody else will do it for you. Sure, they can help and they can remind you of it, but in the end, you're the person in charge of your very own health and wellbeing.

You are the one who has to choose to stop working weekends, to go to bed earlier, and to turn the midnight Netflix marathon off. You are the one who has to make the effort to exercise daily, to drink enough water, and to eat nutritiously.

You know when you need to rest and you know you come back so much stronger after it. You know when you need to give yourself some self-love and you know it makes you happier and more successful in the long run.[47]

This nurturing of yourself can really be anything that helps you to feel better. It could be some form of exercise, a specific meal, or a self-care ritual, like an aromatherapy bath or a full body massage. It could be an afternoon nap or ten minutes of meditation.

Whatever it is, do it. Because you only have one body and being, and you need to treat it as the beautiful temple it is.

Homework:
That's why today's homework is this:

Do one act of self-care today.

For the record, taking a shower or brushing your teeth doesn't count. I'm talking about something with a bit more oomph that you perhaps don't do that often. For example, for me, it's a long hot bath, a facial mask, or some yin yoga stretches. Other times, it's sitting outside in nature, watching the sunset, or picking up a feel-good book.

Your act of self-care can be anything that nurtures you, fuels you, or enriches you in some way. Hence, choose one act of self-care right here right now that you promise to do today - and go and do it.

Always remember to nurture your body and being, and enjoy the relaxation and peace that comes with it.

Day 27:

Find Time to Be Still

"When happiness is present,
you have everything."

~ Epicurus ~

These wise words by philosopher Epicurus really soothe my soul. Simply reading them brings me to the present and makes me appreciate where I am.

His words remind you that you need to be present in the present to experience happiness, regardless of whether you think it's there or not.[48] If it is, and you're too busy looking for it in another shape or form, you will miss it. And, even when you think it's not there, it always is.

That's why it's even more important for you to bring yourself to the present moment and find contentment in it. This is only possible if you learn to slow down and to simply be.

We live increasingly frantic lives. Our stresses just keep on adding up and our smartphones don't give us a moment of peace. We're often running from one place to another, sometimes even trying to multitask whilst we run. All this is making us blind to contentment - and it has to stop.

You need to consciously choose to stop rushing around. You need to consciously choose to simply be. Because if you don't, you're going to wake up one day and wonder where your life went. You really don't want that to happen.

You are a human *being*, not a human *doing*. The answer lies in that word: *being*. Remember that.

Homework:

Going from being to doing, I am still going to ask you to do something today as homework. Why? Because I want you to start this practice of simply being today. Here's how:

Pick one moment today to just be.

Put this moment in your calendar if you need the accountability that comes with it to make it happen. Alternatively, let the moment come to you naturally. Either way, make sure the moment does happen.

In this moment, you should simply be. You shouldn't be observing, meditating, or reading. You shouldn't even be sipping your tea, coffee or juice. Ideally, you should literally just be.

Keep this moment of being at least for one minute - and much longer if you are able to and wish to. If you find yourself feeling agitated, impatient, or annoyed, let those feelings come and go. Then, just continue to be.

Sit on your sofa. Lie on the grass. Stand in the sunshine. It doesn't matter where or how you do it, as long as you are just being. Be in the moment without an agenda, without something to do, and without something to think about.

Learn to simply be, and let happiness catch up with you. Stop your frantic rushing around and stop getting dizzy from all the doing.

Simply... just... be.

Day 28:

Let Go

"Sometimes letting go is an act of far greater power than defending or holding on."

~ Eckhart Tolle ~

Today, I am starting with these wise words of Eckhart Tolle. Why? Because you carry a lot of crap with you.

Just to be clear, I'm not talking about physical crap, like books and clothes or whatever it is that you have in your bag or in your house. I'm talking about what you carry in your mind and in your body.

Thoughts, beliefs, past emotions, past experiences - sometimes you carry so much with you I wonder how you're able to still stand tall. You know that one of the only constants of human life is constant change, yet sometimes you find it hard to move one. You know that not much is stationary, yet sometimes you try to stay stationary yourself.

Somehow, you have a natural desire to hold on to things to try to make them last longer. Maybe you're holding on to something that used to give you pleasure but no longer does. Maybe it's a feeling you know so well you're afraid you'll feel lost without it. Maybe it's a person who's played a big part in your past but doesn't seem to have a role in your present or future. Maybe it's a grudge from a negative interaction that does nothing except prevent that relationship from healing.

Holding on to things prevent you from moving forward, and from becoming who you're meant to be. Holding on to things, and refusing to let go, holds your happiness and your life back.[49] The more you hold on to things, the heavier they become, and the harder it is to let go of them. That's why you need to stop right now. Let go and stop holding on. For your sake, for the sake of the people around you, and for the sake of the world.

Stop letting old, unnecessary crap weigh you down. Let go of the things you no longer need. Let go of the thoughts that hold you back. Let go of the emotions that bring you down. Let go of the people that drown you. Let go of the guilt of your past mistakes. Let go of the need to be constantly busy. Let go of the desire to be perfect.

Just let it all go. Let it go.

Homework:

Fortunately, I'm not going to leave you hanging there and expect you to just magically let it all go. Instead, I'm going to give you a variation of an amazing exercise I learned from one of my spiritual teachers, Susannah Conway.[50]

Before we get started, you need a few things to complete today's homework:

- Pen or pencil
- Lots of post-it notes or small pieces of paper you can write on
- A bin
- Twenty minutes of uninterrupted me time

Once you've got all of the above items, and you know you've got at least twenty minutes to yourself, you can get started:

1. Set a timer for ten minutes and start the clock.
2. Write down everything that you want to let go of today. Give each thought, belief, item, person, or whatever it is that you want to let go of, their own note or piece of paper.
3. Keep writing until the timer runs out.
When it does, you should have a pile of notes, each one with one thing that you are ready to let go of today.
4. Pick up one of the notes, read it out loud, and say, "I'm ready to let go of you today". Then, crumple the paper up, and throw it in the bin.
Repeat this process for every note until all of your notes are crumpled up in the bin.
5. Take the bin out and say goodbye to it for good.

Take a moment to feel how you've cleansed your soul. Sure, some of the things you have written might not disappear immediately. However, you've made a conscious effort to say they are no longer welcome and you've announced to the universe you're ready to let go of them. That is what matters the most and carries the most power in itself.

Feel free to repeat this exercise however often you want. Now go and do it for real - and let go of the things that hold your happiness back.

Day 29:

Reflect

*"Life is a mirror and will reflect back
to the thinker what he thinks into it."*

~ *Ernest Holmes* ~

These wise words from Ernest Holmes really make this stick: reflection, in itself, is the truth. Making the time to reflect gets you closer to the truth.[51] Yet, we struggle, or perhaps forget, to make the time to do this.

If you're being honest, when was the last time you took five minutes to reflect? For me, it was a week ago. And that's only because now I know how important it is. When I didn't, I probably went months, if not longer, without doing any reflecting.

Something that really incentivised me to reflect was the concept of time. You have probably heard the phrase, *"time flies"*, and you might have felt it too. It's when seconds turn into minutes, minutes into hours, hours into days, and, before you know it, years have gone by.

This speeding of time makes it hard to make the time to stop and to take the time to reflect. Which is why today I want you to do exactly that. I want you to do it right now, right here, with me, before we even dive into your homework.

Start by taking a deep breath. Inhale through your nose, exhale through your mouth... Take another deep breath. Inhale... and exhale... Give your shoulders a little shake and gently roll them up and down in circular motions to release any tension in them. Stretch your arms if they're feeling a bit tight. Scrunch up your face and then release it. Keep taking deep breaths.

Then, sit still. Just listen to your breath. When you feel ready, look back on your previous year. Look back on the last 12 months of your life.

Then, ask yourself: *What were your proudest achievements?* What were you most proud of? A new job, a new move, or a new fitness regime? Starting a new relationship, standing up for yourself, or letting go of a belief that was holding you back? Or, maybe, it's having had the courage to read this book – or another one – and live life more fully. Or maybe it's saying yes to marrying the person of your dreams or strengthening the bond with someone you love. Whatever those achievements may be, acknowledge them right now and smile. Be proud of them. Be proud of yourself.

Next, I want you to keep looking back on your past year, and ask yourself: *What were your biggest lessons?* Don't be afraid to look at your mistakes or the setbacks you faced. Make peace with them now. What did you learn from them? How did you become a better person as a result? Acknowledge those moments and remind yourself of the lessons. Smile, and say thank you for them.

Now, for the final question: *What were your most beautiful moments?* A moment of being one with nature? A moment of true love with your partner? A moment of truth in a moment of doubt? Whatever they were, reflect back on them. Feel the beauty that comes with imagining them, and let them energise your soul. Take a deep breath and smile one more time.

How did that feel? Good, I hope. I know it was sweet and short, but hopefully, it was enough to whet your appetite for reflecting more.

Homework:

If you want to practice reflecting even further, I encourage you to go and spend more time reflecting on these questions. You can journal about them, draw about them, talk about them, or simply think about them. Do whatever you need to do to reflect in the most effective way.

Just to recap, the three questions are:

What were your proudest achievements in the last 12 months?

What were your biggest lessons?

What were your most beautiful moments?

Reflect without judgement, reflect without wishing for a certain outcome, and reflect without any reservations. Reflect with kindness and appreciation.

Most importantly, reflect with love.

Day 30:

Listen to Your Heart

"The heart has reasons that
reason does not understand."

~ Blaise Pascal ~

The time has come for me to share my final happiness
tip with you. The incredible quote by Blaise Pascal above
introduces what it's about: listening to your heart.

You can call it listening to your heart, to your
intuition, or to your gut. In the end, it's all insinuating
the same thing: connecting to your inner wisdom and
letting it guide you. To keep it simple, I'll call it
intuition, but feel free to call it whatever you want.

Being able to connect to your intuition, to actually
hear it, and to then also listen to it, makes it easier for
happiness to happen.[52] I strongly believe in this now, but
I have to admit I always haven't.

I didn't really believe there was such a thing as
intuition and, as a result, I also didn't listen to it. For a
long time, it was a conflicting topic for me because I am
a positive psychology practitioner and, hence, I base
most of my work on science. Intuition, however, is a

concept that conflicts with science because it can't be seen, measured, or researched. It's something that is simply felt deep down.

But, before I learned to feel it, or even allowed myself to feel it, I totally numbed it out. I never listened to it and, hence, it turned itself off. It stopped voicing itself or trying to give me guidance. It completely disappeared.

So there I was, living my mediocre, unfulfilling life without my intuition. I kept doubting myself and what I wanted. I stayed stuck in toxic relationships in which I was pretending to be someone who I wasn't. And I didn't even realise it.

What jolted me back to reality, and back to my intuitive voice, was a proposal. The man I was living with asked me to marry him. I figured that was the next natural step in the relationship and, hence, I said yes. That's when my intuition woke up. But I still tried to ignore it.

We set the date, we planned the wedding, and we sent out the invites. The closer the wedding date came, the more my intuition shouted. Yet, I continued to pretend it didn't exist. That's when my intuition took matters into its own hands.

It brought physical symptoms into my body, making me unable to eat, sleep, or focus. It turned my life upside down. I saw my weight drop and any ounce of energy left my body. After weeks of this, I met up with a good friend I hadn't seen for a while. She asked about the wedding plans – which caused me to burst into tears. My intuition had had enough.

I couldn't hide from my truth anymore and I finally opened the door to my intuition. I knew I wasn't meant to marry this man and this was the first time I openly admitted it. I finally listened to every word that my heart had to say and I saw the truth that I could no longer ignore.

I realised I had become someone else. I had become someone that he had wanted me to become. I had lost my real self and disconnected from my most meaningful values. I was living somebody else's life. Knowing that truth is what set me free. Knowing that truth is what gave me the guts to go ahead with the next steps.

I cancelled the wedding, I left the relationship, and I reconnected to who I truly was. For the first time ever, I felt like I was present. That's when I learned the biggest lesson that I could ever learn: the heart knows things that your mind will never know.

Listen to it. It is that voice that will lead you to your happiest, truest life. It is that voice that will help you feel more fulfilment and love.

Don't wait for an alarm to go off to reconnect with your intuition. Choose to reconnect with it right now. Wake it up, and connect with it with every cell in your body and soul. Ask for its guidance and listen to what it has to say. The more you ask, the more it will tell you, and the easier it will be for you to hear it.

As with most things, practice makes perfect and repetition turns it into a habit. Turn listening to your heart into a perfect habit.

Homework:

Start listening to your intuition today. Here's how:

1. Pick one decision you're struggling with right now.

2. Think about the decision and close your eyes.

3. Put your hand on your heart and say:

"This is what's important. What does my heart say?"

It can be as simple as that. Be patient, be persistent, and let the answers come to you. Don't get frustrated if they don't immediately shout out.

Give it time because if you've locked away your intuition like I did, it's going to take some work to get it out again. Simply keep repeating this exercise whenever in doubt.

Just put your hand on your heart, and say: *"This is what's important. What does my heart say?"*

Conclusion:

Continue Your Journey

*"Ever since happiness heard your name,
it has been running through the streets
trying to find you."*

~ Hafiz ~

Your happiness journey doesn't end here. This is only the beginning. Keep revisiting these tips and practising them. The more you do them, the more you'll experience inner fulfilment and the more happiness will organically come your way.

Thank you from the bottom of my heart for reading this. Writing these tips has taken me on a journey of nostalgia, as I've been reminded of my journey of happiness. You have made this so fulfilling and fun, and I hope you have felt the same.

Good luck on your adventures and until next time!

Sending you light, love and happiness,

x Susanna

About the Author:

Susanna Halonen is the Happyologist®, a happiness life coach, motivational speaker, and writer. She is on a mission to make the world a happier place. She wants to help you to kill your self-doubt, to embrace positive thinking, and to build a lifestyle you love.

She holds a Master of Science in Applied Positive Psychology, also known as the science of happiness and human performance, from the University of East London, and a life coaching accreditation from the ICA.

She is the author of *Screw Finding Your Passion* and *Happiness is Here*. She is a published researcher, a TEDx speaker, and a regular commentator in the media from the BBC to The Huffington Post and more. Her corporate client list ranges across industries, including American Express®, Brainwash Festival, BMW, Kellogg's, Lululemon Athletica, and 20th Century Fox Home Entertainment to name a few.

In her free time, she is a competitive dressage rider with Olympic ambitions. She adores dogs and believes we can learn a lot from our four-legged furry friends.

Connect with the Author:
   Website: *www.happyologist.co.uk*
   Instagram: *@TheHappyologist*
   Twitter: *@TheHappyologist*
   Facebook: *facebook.com/thehappyologist*
   YouTube: *youtube.com/c/TheHappyologist*

Recommended Reading:

If you want to dive deeper into your happiness journey, here is my recommended reading list:

Section 1: Happiness 101
The Happiness Advantage by Shawn Achor
The How of Happiness by Sonja Lyubomirsky

Section 2: Your Unique Happiness
Daring Greatly by Brené Brown
Screw Finding Your Passion by Susanna Halonen

Section 3: Your Perspective
Learned Optimism by Martin E. P. Seligman
Mindset by Carol Dweck

Section 4: Your Relationships
How to Win Friends and Influence People by Dale Carnegie
Love 2.0 by Barbara L. Fredrickson

Section 5: Your Body
Presence by Amy Cuddy
Spark by Dr John J. Ratey, Eric Hagerman, & John Ratey

Section 6: Making Your Happiness Last
Self Compassion by Kristin Neff
You Are Here by Thich Nhat Hanh

Cheat Sheet:

Here is a list of the 30 tips I shared with you in this book:

PART I: HAPPINESS 101
Day 01: Why is Happiness Important?
1. Think of a time when you felt really, really happy. What were you doing? What were you seeing? Hearing? Feeling?
2. Now imagine what happened next. How did you perform when you were feeling happy? How did you perform after you felt this happiness?

Day 02: What is Happiness?
1. What are three things that give you any type of positive emotion? What are three things that make you feel good?
2. Do one of the positive emotion boosting activities today. If you can't do exactly that, do the next best closest possible thing.
3. How can you incorporate more of these positive emotion boosting activities into your daily life?

Day 03: What Is Not Happiness? - Part I
1. Whenever you notice a negative emotion today, simply become aware of it. Don't try to fight it, resist it, deny it or change it. Simply notice it.
2. Give a label to the negative emotion you feel. Call it

stress, or fear, or anxiety, or whatever it is that you are feeling.

3. Say, "*I feel stressed*", or "*I feel anxious*". Basically, say, "*I feel X*", and fill X with the specific negative emotion that you are experiencing in that moment.

Day 04: What Is Not Happiness? - Part II

1. When you come across a problem today, talk to it. Say to it: "*Everything is fleeting, including you.*" Simply notice the problem and accept its impermanence.

2. Notice how you feel when you are doing this. The most common reaction is to experience more of a sense of calm and confidence when you voice out loud that the problem is fleeting.

3. Ask yourself: What can I do to diminish this problem – or - turn my attitude into a more positive one when it comes to dealing with it?

Day 05: How Do You Reach Happiness?

1. What is one thing you can do to remind yourself to choose happiness daily?

2. What can you do to remember not to chase happiness in the shape of destinations?

PART II: YOUR UNIQUE HAPPINESS

Day 06: Connect with Your Authentic Self

1. When do you feel most like yourself?

When do you feel really true to who you are? When do

you feel like you can really show up fully? What environments encourage you to be real?

2. Why? Why do these situations bring your real self out?

What is it about them that makes it possible? What is it that gives you the courage to be you in these situations?

Day 07: Discover Your Values

1. What are your top three values?

Think about the principles you want to live your life by. What are the non-negotiable ones for you?

2. How are you living life in alignment with them now?

What are you doing in your life already that is aligned with your values?

3. How could you live your life more in alignment with your values?

Day 08: Realise Your Why

1. Why do you do what you do?

Think both big and small. Think of your overarching life purpose. Also, think of all the little things you do daily and what their why's are.

2. Then, challenge yourself by asking: How can you have even more purpose in your life? What can you do to connect with your life purpose more powerfully? What can you do to connect to all the little actions you do daily in a more meaningful way?

Day 09: Embrace Your Strengths

1. What are your top three strengths?

Get real here about the actual human strengths you have.

2. How could you use your strengths in new, different ways?

Day 10: Unlock Your Passion

1. When do you feel you are most passionate and energetic?

2. How can you bring more of that passion into other areas of your life?

PART III: YOUR PERSPECTIVE
Day 11: Be Grateful

What are three specific things you are most grateful for in the last 24 hours?

Day 12: Practice Optimism

1. Pick a problem or a challenge you have.

(If you can't think of any right now, make one up!)

2. Talk about the problem as if you were a pessimist.

i.e. The problem is permanent, all-encompassing, and all my fault.

3. Switch to the other side and talk about it as if you were an optimist.

i.e. The problem is fleeting, it's only this thing rather than my whole life, and there are multiple variables at play, hence, it's not a reflection of me or my abilities.

4. Reflect on the two states of mind you tested out. Which one of them makes you feel more empowered?

Day 13: Notice the Beauty

1. Look up from this page into your surroundings.

2. What can you see around you that is beautiful?

Day 14: Do Something Challenging

What is one thing you can do today that challenges you?

Day 15: Choose Resilience

1. Think of a time when you were faced with a setback or experienced some sort of failure that felt difficult to overcome.

2. How is your life - or how are you - better because of it?

How is your life or how are you better because of this setback?

PART IV: YOUR RELATIONSHIPS

Day 16: Connect

Who are the people that energise you, encourage you, and believe in you - sometimes more than you believe in yourself?

Who are the people who love you for who you are and encourage you to show up authentically every single day?

Day 17: Be Kind

Do three random acts of kindness today.

Day 18: Celebrate

1. Pick someone in your life to give thanks to.

Pick anyone you want and get ready to give a heartfelt thank you to them.

2. Tell them what they mean to you. Tell them what you admire and appreciate about them the most. Do this through a face-to-face conversation, a phone call, an email, or even a letter.

Day 19: Declutter

Ask yourself: Does this person give me joy?

If the answer is no, limit your interactions with them, try to inject more joy into your relationship, or, ultimately, let them go.

Day 20: Love

Say this to someone you love: "*I love you*".

PART V: YOUR BODY

Day 21: Breathe

1. Inhale through your nose for four counts.

2. Hold your breath for seven counts.

3. Exhale through relaxed, pressed lips for eight counts.

4. Repeat again and again until you start to feel the relaxation.

Day 22: Smile

Smile at three strangers today.

Day 23: Hug
Give someone a 20-second hug today.

Day 24: Power Pose
1. Stand up.
2. Put your feet firmly on the ground and have them a little bit wider than your hips.
3. Straighten your posture, push your chest out, and lift your chin.
4. Put your hand firmly on your hips - or high above your head straight towards the sky.
5. Hold the pose for two minutes. Remember to keep on breathing.

Day 25: Move
Move at least three times today, and, for 10 minutes each of those times.

PART VI: MAKING YOUR HAPPINESS LAST
Day 26: Nurture Yourself
Do one act of self-care today.

Day 27: Find Time to Be Still
Pick one moment today to just be.

Day 28: Let Go
1. Set a timer for ten minutes and start the clock.
2. Write down everything that you want to let go of today.

Give each thought, belief, item, person, or whatever it is that you want to let go of, their own note or piece of paper.

3. Keep writing until the timer runs out.

When it does, you should have a pile of notes, each one with one thing that you are ready to let go of today.

4. Pick up one of the notes, read it out loud, and say, *"I'm ready to let go of you today"*. Then, crumple the paper up and throw it in the bin.

Repeat this process for every note until all of your notes are crumpled up in the bin.

5. Take the bin out and say goodbye to it for good.

Day 29: Reflect

What were your proudest achievements in the last 12 months?

What were your biggest lessons?

What were your most beautiful moments?

Day 30: Listen to Your Heart

1. Pick one decision you're struggling with right now.

2. Think about the decision and close your eyes.

3. Put your hand on your heart and say:

"This is what's important. What does my heart say?"

References:

PART I:

[1] Achor, Shawn (2013). *Before Happiness: Five Actionable Strategies to Create a Positive Path to Success*. New York: The Random House Group.

[2] Lyubomirsky, Sonja, and Porta, Matthew D. Della. (2012). Boosting Happiness, Buttressing Resilience. In John W. Reich, Alex Zautra and John Stuart Hall (ed), *Handbook of Adult Resilience* (p.450-464). New York: Guildford Press.

[3] Diener, Ed, and Seligman, Martin E. P. (2002). Very Happy People. *Psychological Science, 13*(1), 81-84.

[4] Lyubomirsky, Sonja, King, Laura, and Diener, Ed (2005). The benefits of frequent positive affect: Does happiness lead to success? *Psychological Bulletin, 131*(6), 803-855.

[5] Veenhoven, Ruut (2008). Healthy happiness: effects of happiness on physical health and the consequences for preventive health care. *Journal of Happiness Studies, 9*(3), 449-469.

[6] Achor, Shawn (2010). *The Happiness Advantage: The Seven Principles of Positive Psychology that Fuel Success and Performance at Work*. New York, NY: Crown Business.

Estrada, Carlos, Isen, Alice M., & Young, Mark J. (1994). Positive affect influences creative problem solving and reported source of practice satisfaction in physicians. *Motivation and Emotion, 18*(4), 285–299.

[7] Ryan, Richard M. & Deci, Edward L. (2001). On happiness and human potentials: A review of research on hedonic and

eudaimonic wellbeing. *Annual Review of Psychology, 52*(1), 141–166.

[8] Margolis, Rachel, and Myrskylä, Mikko. (2015). Parental well-being surrounding first birth as a determinant of further parity progression. *Demography, 52*(4), 1147-1166.

Nelson, S. Katherine, Kushlev, Kostadin, English, Tammy, Dunn, Elizabeth W., & Lyubomirsky, Sonja (2012). In defence of parenthood: Children are associated with more joy than misery. *Psychological Science,* 24(1), 3–10.

[9] Style, Charlotte (2011). *Brilliant Positive Psychology: What makes us happy, optimistic and motivated.* Harlow: Pearson Education Limited.

[10] Style, Charlotte (2011). *Brilliant Positive Psychology: What makes us happy, optimistic and motivated.* Harlow: Pearson Education Limited.

[11] Dweck, Carol (2006). *Mindset: The New Psychology of Success.* New York: Random House, Inc.

[12] Achor, Shawn (2010). *The Happiness Advantage: The Seven Principles of Positive Psychology that Fuel Success and Performance at Work.* New York, NY: Crown Business.

[13] Lyubomirsky, Sonja (2007). *The How of Happiness: a practical guide to getting what you want.* London: Sphere.

PART II:

[14] Ryan, Richard M. & Deci, Edward L. (2001). On happiness and human potentials: A review of research on hedonic and eudaimonic wellbeing. *Annual Review of Psychology,* 52(1), 141–166.

[15] Sagiv, Lilah, Roccas, Sonia, & Hazan, Ostnat (2004). Value

pathways to well-being: Healthy values, valued goal attainment and environmental congruence. In P. A. Linley and S. Joseph (eds.), *Positive Psychology in Practice*. Hoboken, NJ: John Wiley and Sons, pp.68–84.

[16] Baumeister, Roy F., & Vohs, Kathleen D. (2005). Meaningfulness in life. In C. R. Snyder and S. J. Lopez (eds.), *Handbook of Positive Psychology*. Oxford: Oxford University Press, p.614

[17] Baumeister, Roy F., & Vohs, Kathleen D. (2005). Meaningfulness in life. In C. R. Snyder and S. J. Lopez (eds.), *Handbook of Positive Psychology*. Oxford: Oxford University Press, p.614

[18] Gallup (10 May 1999). Item 8: My Company's Mission or Purpose. *Gallup Business Journal Online*. Retrieved from: http://businessjournal.gallup.com/content/505/item-8-my-companys-mission-or-purpose.aspx

[19] Asplund, Jim (27 September 2012). When Americans Use Their Strengths More, They Stress Less. *Gallup Wellbeing Online*. Retrieved online from: http://www.gallup.com/poll/157679/americans-strengths-stress-less.aspx

[20] Seligman, Martin E. P., Park, Nansook & Peterson, Chris (2004). The Values In Action (VIA) classification of character strengths. *Ricerche di Psicologia*, 27(1), 63–78.

[21] Linley, Alex, Nielsen, Karina M., Wood, Alex M., Gillett, Raphael, and Biswas-Diener, Robert. (2010). Using signature strengths in the pursuit of goals: Effects on goal progress, need satisfaction, and well-being, and implications for coaching psychologists. *International Coaching Psychology Review*, 5(1), 6–15.

[22] Halonen, Susanna & Lomas, Tim (2014). The passionate way of being: The promises and perils of entering the passion spiral. *International Journal of Psychological Research, 7*(2), 17-28.

PART III:

[23] Wood, Alex M., Froh, Jeffrey J., and Geraghty, Adam W. A. (2010). Gratitude and well-being: A review and theoretical integration. *Clinical Psychology Review, 30*(7), 890-905.

[24] Seligman, Martin E. P., Steen, Tracy A., Park, Nansook, and Peterson, Christopher. (2005). Positive psychology progress: Empirical validation of interventions. *American Psychologist, 60*(5), 410-421.

[25] Carver, Charles, and Scheier, Michael (2005). Optimism. In Charles R. Snyder and Shane J. Lopez (eds), *Handbook of Positive Psychology*. Oxford: Oxford University Press, p.235.

[26] Seligman, Martin E.P. (2006). *Learned Optimism: How to change your mind and your life.* First Vintage Books ed. New York: Random House.

[27] Lyubomirsky, Sonja (2007). *The How of Happiness: a practical guide to getting what you want.* London: Sphere.

Sheldon, Kennon M. and Kasser, Tim (1998). Pursuing personal goals: Skills enable progress, but not all progress is beneficial. *Personality and Social Psychology Bulletin, 24*(12), 1319-1331.

[28] Dweck, Carol (2006). *Mindset: The New Psychology of Success.* New York: Random House, Inc.

[29] Tugade, Michele M., and Fredrickson, Barbara L. (2004). Resilient Individuals Use Positive Emotions to Bounce Back

From Negative Emotional Experiences. *Journal of Personality and Social Psychology, 88* (2), 320-333.

PART IV:

[30] Robison, Jennifer (2011). Happiness is love – and $75,000: Two researchers uncover what really makes people happy: friends and money (though you don't have to be rich to be happy). *Gallup Management Journal.* Retrieved online from: http://ultimatecoachuniversity.com/wp-content/uploads/2011/09/UCU-Finding-the-What-and-the-Why-Part-2-Article.pdf

[31] Mongrain, Myriam, Chin, Jacqueline M., and Shapira, Leah B. (2011). Practicing compassion increases happiness and self-esteem. *Journal of Happiness Studies, 12*(6), 963-981.

[32] Gordon, Cameron L., Arnette, Robyn A. M., and Smith, Rachel E. (2011). Have you thank your spouse today?: Felt and expressed gratitude among married couples. *Personality and Individual Differences, 50*(3), 339-343.

[33] Style, Charlotte (2011). *Brilliant Positive Psychology: What makes us happy, optimistic and motivated.* Harlow: Pearson Education Limited.

[34] Kondo, Marie (2014). *The Life-Changing Magic of Tidying: A simple, effective way to banish clutter forever.* London: Vermilion.

[35] Fredrickson, Barbara (2014). *Love 2.0: Finding happiness and health in moments of connection.* London: Penguin Group.

PART V:

[36] Seppälä, Emma (2016). TEDxSacramento talk titled

'Breathing Happiness' by Emma Seppälä. Retrieved online from: https://emmaseppala.com/tedxtalk-breathing-happiness/

[37] Weil, Dr Andrew (2016). *4-7-8 Breathing: Health Benefits & Demonstration.* Retrieved online from: https://www.drweil.com/videos-features/videos/the-4-7-8-breath-health-benefits-demonstration/

[38] Mulder, Patty (2012). *Communication Model by Albert Mehrabian.* Retrieved online from ToolsHero: https://www.toolshero.com/communication-skills/communication-model-mehrabian/

[39] Li, Ding (2014). *What's the science behind a smile?* Retrieved online from: https://www.britishcouncil.org/voices-magazine/famelab-whats-science-behind-smile

[40] Li, Ding (2014). *What's the science behind a smile?* Retrieved online from: https://www.britishcouncil.org/voices-magazine/famelab-whats-science-behind-smile

[41] Guerreiro, Susana (2017). Oxytocin: from biology to love. *Endocrine Abstracts, 49,* S28.2. Retrieved online from: http://www.endocrine-abstracts.org/ea/0049/ea0049S28.2.htm

[42] Guerreiro, Susana (2017). Oxytocin: from biology to love. *Endocrine Abstracts, 49,* S28.2. Retrieved online from: http://www.endocrine-abstracts.org/ea/0049/ea0049S28.2.htm

[43] Harvard Health Publishing (2014). *Hugs heartfelt in more ways than one.* Retrieved online from: https://www.health.harvard.edu/newsletter_article/In_brief_Hugs_heartfelt_in_more_ways_than_one

[44] TED.com (2012). Talk titled "*Your body language may shape who you are*" by Amy Cuddy. Retrieved online from:

https://www.ted.com/talks/amy_cuddy_your_body_language_shapes_who_you_are

[45] Cuddy, Amy (2016). *Presence: Bringing Your Boldest Self to Your Biggest Challenges.* London: Orion.

[46] Dunstan, David W., Kingwell, Bronwyn A., Larsen, Robyn, Healy, Genevieve N., Hamilton, Marc T., Shaw, Jonathan E., Bertovic, David A., Zimmet, Paul Z., Salmon, Jo and Owen, Neville. (2012). Breaking up prolonged sitting reduces postprandial glucose and insulin responses. *Diabetes Care, 35*(5), 976-983.

PART VI:

[47] Neff, Kristin (2011). *Self Compassion: Stop beating yourself up and leave insecurity behind.* New York: HarperCollins.

[48] Brown, Kirk W., Ryan, Richard M. (2003). The benefits of being present: Mindfulness and its role in psychological well-being. *Journal of Personality and Social Psychology, 84*(4), 822-848.

[49] McCullough, Michael E. (2001). Forgiveness: Who does it and how do they do it? *Current Directions in Psychological Science, 10*(6), 194-197.

[50] Conway, Susannah (2017). Retrieved from her blog at: http://www.susannahconway.com/

[51] Style, Charlotte and Boniwell, Ilona (2010). The effect of group-based life coaching on happiness and well-being. *Groupwork, 20*(3), 51-72.

[52] Halonen, Susanna (2015). *3 Reasons Why You Have to Trust Your Gut.* Retrieved from Psychology Today online: https://www.psychologytoday.com/blog/the-path-passionate-

happiness/201505/3-reasons-why-you-have-trust-your-gut?collection=1074680